Who was the Prophet ELISHA?

ISRAEL DRAZIN

Who was the Prophet ELISHA?

gefen
publishing house ‏בית ההוצאה לאור‏ ‏גפן‏
JERUSALEM ◆ NEW YORK   Est. 1981

Cover Design: Leah Ben Avraham/Noonim Graphics
Illustration used with the kind permission of the estate of the late Angus McBride
Typesetting: www.optumetech.com

ISBN: 978-965-7801-60-4

Gefen Books
c/o Baker & Taylor Publisher Services
30 Amberwood Parkway
Ashland, Ohio 44805
516-593-1234
orders@gefenpublishing.com

Gefen Publishing House Ltd.
6 Hatzvi Street
Jerusalem 9438614,
Israel
972-2-538-0247
orders@gefenpublishing.com

www.gefenpublishing.com

Printed in Israel

Library of Congress Control Number: 2024938963

Note

The translations of the Bible and the Hebrew commentaries are my translations. All of the comments on the text are mine except when I indicate the source.

My approach in this book and my other books is to see what the Bible says, not what we want it to say. Readers should not think I criticize Elisha, the Torah, or traditional Jewish law. I am an Orthodox observant Jew. But what I discovered in my study is surprising.

I kept the notes in this book to a minimum, usually very short and only to indicate the source of the opinion cited. It is only rarely that I use the note to give additional information. Readers can read the text without looking at the notes.

The cover photograph of this book is a painting by Angus McBride depicting a Hittite chariot. While the painter may not have had Elisha in mind, the picture depicts the honor bestowed upon him by the king of Israel while Elisha was about to die after more than sixty years of service to Israel. The king described him as *"the chariot of Israel and its horsemen."* The king referred to Israel's enemy country, Moab, which had many war chariots and a large military force, while Israel lacked these physical defenses. Yet, Elisha was a better chariot and horseman than Israel's foe. His advice to Israel during his more than sixty years made Israel capable of defeating Moab.

Dedicated as usual with love to my wife Dina, my inspiration
who makes it possible for me to write books and articles
She is superb. We have been married 64 years.

Fifty books by Israel Drazin

Maimonides and Rational Series
Maimonides: Reason Above All
Maimonides and the Biblical Prophets
Maimonides: The Extraordinary Mind
A Rational Approach to Judaism and Torah Commentary
Naḥmanides: An Unusual Thinker
What we Don't Know about God and people in the Hebrew Bible: Genesis
What we Don't Know about God and people in the Hebrew Bible: Exodus
What we Don't Know About God and the people in the Bible: Leviticus
What we Don't Know About God and the people in the Bible: Numbers
What We Don't Know About God and the People in the Bible: Deuteronomy

Mysteries of Judaism
Mysteries of Judaism I
Mysteries of Judaism II: How the Rabbis and Others Changed Judaism
Mysteries of Judaism III: Common Sense Evaluations of Religious Thoughts
Mysteries of Judaism IV: Over 100 Mistaken Ideas about God and the Bible
Mysteries of Judaism V: More than 150 Mistaken Ideas about God and the Bible Stories that Teach the Truth

Unusual Bible Interpretation series
Five Books of Moses
Joshua
Judges
Ruth, Esther, and Judith
Jonah and Amos
Hosea

Other Books on the Bible
Who Was the Biblical Samuel?
The Tragedies of King David
Who Really Was the Biblical David?
The Authentic King Solomon

Who Really Was the Biblical Elijah?
Who Was the Prophet Elisha?

Scholarly Targum Books:
Targumic Studies
Targum Onkelos to Exodus
Targum Onkelos to Leviticus
Targum Onkelos to Numbers
Targum Onkelos to Deuteronomy

Novel
She Wanted to Be Jewish

Editor of and forewords to Nathan Drazin's books:
Legends Worth Living
Abraham - The Father of the Jewish People

With Cecil B. Currey:
For God and Country

With Stanley Wagner:
Understanding the Bible Text: Onkelos on the Torah: Genesis
Understanding the Bible Text: Onkelos on the Torah: Exodus
Understanding the Bible Text: Onkelos on the Torah: Leviticus
Understanding the Bible Text: Onkelos on the Torah: Numbers
Understanding the Bible Text: Onkelos on the Torah: Deuteronomy
Understanding Onkelos
Beyond the Bible Text
Iyunim Betargum (Hebrew)

With Leba Lieder
Can't Start Passover without the Bread
Sailing on Moti's Ark on Succoth
Just What the Doctor Ordered: Moti's Purim Story

As Daniel A. Diamond

Around the World in 123 Days

Chaos on the Victoria: Around the World in 78 Days, Almost

Rational Religion

Fifteen forewords to books by Rabbi Dr. Michael Leo Samuel

Maimonides' Hidden Torah Commentary, Genesis, Book One

Maimonides' Hidden Torah Commentary, Genesis, Book Two

Maimonides' Hidden Torah Commentary, Exodus, Book One

Maimonides' Hidden Torah Commentary, Exodus, Book Two

Maimonides' Hidden Torah Commentary, Leviticus

Maimonides' Hidden Torah Commentary, Numbers

Maimonides' Hidden Torah commentary, Deuteronomy

An Odyssey of Faith

Gentle Jewish wisdom

Birth and Rebirth Through Genesis 1–11

Birth and Rebirth Through Genesis 12–27

Kabbalah Demystified

A Shepherd's Song: Psalm 23

A Shepherd's Song: Psalm 23, second edition

Of Lions, Mice, and Menorahs, A Jewish Look at Aesop's Fables

Contents

Acknowledgments

Thanks to Fern Seckbach for preparing the index, and to Ruth Pepperman who did the final checking and proofreading of this book.

Introduction

In 2020 I finished my book *Who Really Was the Biblical Prophet Elijah?* by noting that Kings[1] unfavorably describes Elijah and concludes with a depiction of God taking him to heaven, symbolically representing his death. God killed him to stop him from continuing to criticize Israel over-zealously. I followed this with the question, why does the ancient Jewish tradition take the opposite approach? It praises Elijah. It states he will return and announce the arrival of the Messiah. I left this question with no good answer.

When I studied Elijah's successor, Elisha, I found the answer. I will reveal it in this book. It will surprise most readers.

But let's start with some background.

FORMER HISTORY

The stories of Elijah and Elisha (who succeeded Elijah as prophet) are told within the tales of the kings of Israel.

Briefly, King David united the twelve Israelite tribes with him as their ruler. We do not know the precise dates of his life, but most scholars date him to 1000 BCE, about 3,000 years ago. David was succeeded by his son Solomon, who angered ten of the twelve tribes. When Solomon died, his son ruled after him. The son told the twelve tribes he would continue the practices of his father. This angered ten of them. They abandoned him and created their kingdom in the north, which they named Israel. Solomon's son and his descendants remained kings over only two tribes in the south, which was called Judea. Jeroboam became king over Israel in 932 BCE. Israel established two temples, which were primarily for idols.

---

1. Christians divided Kings as well as some other books into two parts and Jews accepted the division.

ELIJAH

Elijah and Elisha were apparently born in Israel. While most, but not all of Israel's inhabitants, worshiped idols, the two were vehemently and fiercely opposed to idol worship. They tried to persuade the kings of Israel and their subjects to worship the true God. They existed during the reigns of three kings, beginning with King Ahab of Israel, who assumed the role in 876 BCE to when King Jehu, the fourth Israel king, assassinated the prior king and ruled instead in 843 BCE. The Bible does not give the dates. Those mentioned are from the commentary of Doctor I.W. Slotki to the biblical book of Kings.[2] Not all scholars accept these dates.[3]

Elijah was secretive. No one knew where he lived until he suddenly appeared. Elisha was friendlier. But he was more impatient. People visited Elisha.

The biblical story of Elijah is relatively short. It is in only five chapters (I Kings 17, 18, 19, 21, and II Kings 2). Just 139 verses deal with him. There are also two very suspect brief mentions in two other biblical books. One is II Chronicles 21:12 that states the prophet Elijah sent a letter to a Judean king, not a king of Israel whom Elijah normally addressed, which some scholars insist is not the Elijah of the Book of Kings. The second is in the end of the book Malachi where the man is called Eliyah. I will discuss the second later. Elijah is mentioned in the New Testament in Matthew 17:3-13, Mark 9:4-13, and Luke 9:30-33.

The biblical Elijah was overzealous, more than Elisha. He never really showed interest in helping people. He is different from the Elijah who appears in the legends of post-biblical literature. In the legends, he is kind and generally very friendly to people. God was unsatisfied with the biblical Elijah and criticized and punished him. God killed him.

There were twenty events in which Elijah was involved. Readers differ on whether they were miracles or natural events. Most are easy to explain as natural events. Of those listed below, items 1, 2, 4, 6, 7, 8, 9, 14, 19, and 20 can be easily explained as natural occurrences. For example, Elijah's act of saving the child in item 4 could be considered artificial respiration. Similarly, item 8, that he did not die from not eating and drinking for forty days, could be assumed to be a typical

---

2. Israel Wolf Slotki, *Kings* (London: The Soncino Press, 1950).

3. Some scholars date Ahab from 935 to 852 BCE and date his reign beginning in 874 BCE. His wife was the famed evil Jezebel.

biblical exaggeration. He was able to survive on scant food during this period. Elijah being taken to heaven is more than likely a poetic way of saying he died. Or, more precisely, that God killed him to stop him from mistreating people.

Five behaviors, 10, 11, 12, 13, and 17, called prophecies, could be called predictions based on a keen understanding of events and people. But not communications from God. Although overzealous, Elijah was brilliant.

Five are more challenging to see as natural occurrences. But not impossible. They are 3, 5, 15, 16, and 18. Did God order Elijah to perform the acts? The Bible itself does not say so. The only times that Elijah was ordered by an angel or God to do something was when he was told to go somewhere, and these instructions could be understood as Elijah deciding to move.

I am convinced that two of the five behaviors attributed to Elijah, 15 and 16, belong among the Elisha activities. Elisha, as we will see, was more impatient than Elijah. His impatience caused him to act improperly. When forty-two youngsters insulted him, he caused a bear to kill them. It is not surprising that he would murder a hundred soldiers. True, Elijah killed four hundred Baal priests, but through overzealousness, not impatience. He was prompted by his love of God, not a personal insult. If I am correct, there are only three problematic Elijah practices.

ELIJAH'S ACTIVITIES

1. He prophesied to King Ahab that a drought would last several years (I Kings 17:1).
2. Ravens fed him food (I Kings 17:4).
3. Caused a jar of meal and a cruse of oil not to diminish (I Kings 17:14).
4. Restored life to a child (I Kings 17:22).
5. Brought fire to consume a sacrifice on Mount Carmel (I Kings 18:38).
6. Killed or ordered to be killed hundreds of priests of Baal (I Kings 18:40).
7. Brought rain (I Kings 18:45).
8. Was able to live without eating for forty days (I Kings 19:8).
9. Heard the criticism of his behavior from God while at Mount Sinai (I Kings 19: 11).
10. Prophesied to appoint kings and his successor Elisha (I Kings 19:16).
11. Prophesied that Ahab's sons would die (I Kings 21:22).
12. Prophesied that dogs would devour Jezebel (II Kings 21:23).

13. Prophesied that King Azariah would die (II Kings 1:4).
14. An angel advised him how to act (II Kings 1:15).
15. Called fire to descend from heaven to kill 50 soldiers (II Kings 1:10).
16. Did the same to a second group of 50 soldiers (II Kings 1:12).
17. Prophesied the death of a king (II Kings 1:17).
18. Split the Jordan to create a dry path (II Kings 2:8).
19. Prophesied that Elisha would have a double portion (II Kings 2:10).
20. Ascended to heaven in a fiery chariot with fiery horses in a whirlwind (II Kings 2:11).

ELIJAH AS DEPICTED IN THE BIBLICAL BOOK MALACHI

Almost all of Elijah's acts were performed because of his overzealous love of God and his hatred of idol worship. Those acts not activated because of zeal do not display warm feelings toward others.[4] Yet, the biblical book Malachi is held by many, Jews and non-Jews alike, to prophesy the coming of the prophet Elijah centuries after his death.

Malachi means "my messenger," as seen in Malachi 3:1. Thus, many clerics and scholars of all religions recognize that we cannot know the prophet's name, and rabbis, for example, have made several suggestions. At the end of the book Malachi, the prophet is said to predict the return of Elijah. But this is inconsistent with what he says previously. He did not deal with the messianic age but with a resolution of the problems caused by intermarriage. Malachi states in 3:23 and 24, "Behold, I will send you Eliyah the prophet before that great and dreadful day of the Lord comes. He will turn the hearts of fathers to children and the hearts of children to their fathers, or else I will come and destroy the land." These words have nothing to do with a messianic age. Yet, many people – perhaps driven by hope – contend that Malachi is saying that sometime in the future, Elijah will return and announce the Messiah's coming.

The idea of a revived Elijah returning to announce the arrival of the Messiah, as if there was a need for such an announcement, and the obscure meaning of Elijah being taken to heaven in a whirlwind, which, as previously stated, is most likely a fanciful way of saying he died, led people to believe that Elijah is still

---

4. The only possible exception is when he saved the life (or resurrected) the child of the woman who gave him food and lodging. But even here, Elijah shows no human feelings. He most likely acted because he felt he owed his landlady for helping him.

alive and comes to earth on many occasions to help people. But, as we have seen, this legendary Elijah, who generally helps people in distress, totally differs from the overzealous biblical Elijah with whom God was displeased.

ELISHA

While Elijah's story appears in five chapters, in 139 verses, the drama of Elisha appears in ten chapters, in 206 verses. The first appearance of Elisha is in I Kings 19. The other nine are in II Kings 2, 3, 4, 5, 6, 7, 8, 9, and 13.

Elisha's stories are fascinating. We read how he first appears as a wealthy farmer. However, as is common in scripture, the source of his wealth is obscure. Scripture is obscure in order to prompt us to think. He may have been the son of wealthy parents. We read how he admires Elijah, leaving home to follow him. We see acts he performs similar to those of Moses and Elijah. He starts by helping those close to him, then helps large groups. He then becomes the advisor to the king of Israel. During his final years, he is so respected that even Israel's enemy, the Ammonite king, requests his help.

Most of his acts are beneficial. But Elisha has faults. He is like every person in the Hebrew Bible, not perfect. Even King David, whom Jews, Christians, and Muslims respect, committed adultery and had the woman's husband murdered.

Readers may want to consider as they read this book who of the two prophets was better. Is the Bible preferring Elisha by telling his tale in more detail than that of Elijah, and revealing more "miracles"? Also, does scripture belittle Elijah when it states he was taken to heaven in a chariot, which, as previously stated, could mean God killed him? Additionally, doesn't the Torah, in contrast, extol Elisha after he died by saying that he was so "holy" that touching his dead body resulted in a dead man being restored to life? Yet, Jewish tradition supposes that Elijah will announce the coming of the Messiah. How do we deal with this seeming contradiction? Who was the better prophet?

ARE THE "MIRACLES" OF ELIJAH AND ELISHA NATURAL EVENTS?

There is a greater concentration of miracles in the Elijah and Elisha stories in the biblical book of Kings than in the Exodus tales.[5] Are all of them natural events? Maimonides would answer that they were natural events. In his *Guide for the*

---

5.   J. Robinson, *The First Book of Kings*, The Cambridge Bible Commentary Series (Cambridge: Cambridge University Press) 1972, 191. Robinson, like Ehrlich in his *Mikra Ki-Pheshuto*

Perplexed 2:48, Maimonides emphasizes that whenever the Bible states that an event, including communication, is attributed to God, what occurred did so by natural law. He explained that the matter is attributed to God even though God is not the direct cause because God is the "ultimate cause" since God created or formed the laws of nature. Among many examples, Maimonides includes I Kings 17:9. Although the verse states that God commanded the widow to maintain Elijah, God was not directly involved. Elijah negotiated with the woman.

Nachmanides disagreed. He states in Genesis 17:1, 46:15, Exodus 13:16, and Leviticus 26:11 that this world does not function through the laws of nature. God is constantly and directly involved in every occurrence of humans and matter, frequently interfering with and controlling human thoughts and behavior. He calls the daily unseen divine manipulations "hidden miracles." They contrast with miracles that are, according to him, clearly divine acts, such as the Ten Plagues inflicted on the Egyptians.

For example, he contends that when a Midrash relates that the patriarch Abraham was saved when King Nimrod threatened to kill him, God interfered with nature and changed Nimrod's intention; He "put it in the heart of that king to save him." He used this principle of divine intervention to explain various other Midrashim, which he considered facts, such as the unusual length of the lives of Moses' mother and the behaviors of Aaron's grandson Pinchas and King David's ancestress Ruth.

Other Jewish sages took a middle path. In his Torah commentary, Gersonides agrees with Maimonides in part. He writes that God "generally" prefers that what transpires on earth does so according to the laws of nature. Therefore, he says, God did not save Elijah with a miracle but told Elijah to hide. Abarbanel is like Gersonides. He notes in his commentary that the Bible does not state that God instructed him to do anything until chapter 19, when Elijah came to Mount Sinai, also called Horeb. Elijah instigated everything else. The late Chief Rabbi of the British Empire, Dr. J. H. Hertz, explained in his "Additional Notes" to his excellent commentary, *The Pentateuch and Haftorahs*, that the first nine plagues in Egypt were natural events.[6]

---

states, "The character of the miraculous bears all the characteristics of human folk-tales, rather than the self-revelation of God."

6. J.H. Hertz, *The Pentateuch and Haftorahs*. Additional Notes. (London: Soncino Press, 1972).

In one of my books, I added that the tenth plague was also a natural event. The biblical style emphasizes and even exaggerates events to impress readers. When the Torah states that *all* first-born humans and cattle died, it is informing us that the plagues, which originated from the contaminants that were discharged from the blood of dead Israelite children when Pharaoh ordered his troops to kill male children and toss their bodies into the Nile, spread even to *many* of the most prized humans and animals.

Still others maintain that miracles occurred in the early days of the Israelites because they were closer to God, more intelligent, and more pious than their descendants. However, they were discontinued during the second Temple because the people were no longer sufficiently righteous.

Chapter 1

ELISHA IS CHOSEN AS ELIJAH'S SUCCESSOR

Chapter 19 introduces readers to Elisha. We see him being chosen as Elijah's successor. While the chapter seem straightforward and easy to understand, a closer reading reveals that it is filled with obscurities. Elisha reacts enthusiastically. But his behavior is somewhat strange.

I KINGS CHAPTER 19[1]

15. Y-H-V-H told him [Elijah], "Return the same way you came to the wilderness of Damascus. Anoint Hazael to be king of Aram when you arrive.

16. Then anoint Jehu son of Nimshi to be king of Israel. And anoint Elisha son of Shaphat from Abel-meholah to replace you as prophet.

17. Jehu will kill anyone who escapes the sword of Hazael, and Elisha will kill those who escape the sword of Jehu.

18. Yet I will save 7,000 in Israel who never bowed down to Baal or kissed him."

19. He went and found Elisha son of Shaphat plowing a field. There were twelve teams of oxen before him. Elisha was with the twelfth. Elijah went to him and threw his cloak over him.

20. He left the oxen, ran after Elijah, and asked, "Please let me go and kiss my father and mother goodbye, and then I will go with you!" He replied, "Go back, for what have I done to you?"

21. He left him, took the yoke of oxen, slaughtered them, boiled their flesh with the instruments of the oxen, gave it to the people, and they all ate. Then, he followed Elijah and served him.

---

1. I will introduce each chapter in the biblical book Kings with what the Bible writes and then follow the quote with my understanding.

1

WHAT HAPPENED BEFORE THIS?

In the first part of chapter 19, Ahab tells his wife Jezebel that Elijah killed 450 priests of the idol Baal at Mount Carmel. She is enraged and sends a message to Elijah that she will avenge the death of her priests by killing him. He flees in fear to Mount Sinai and sits in a cave. He has a vision there. God is revealed as a soft-spoken voice, not as a loud, harsh windstorm, a noisy earthquake, or a burning fire. God then ordered him to anoint Elisha as his replacement, which he did, and Elisha followed him as his successor.

We can understand that, fearing an assassination, Elijah ran to Mount Sinai, where God had appeared to Moses, whom he admired. He hoped God would reveal to him that his zealousness for Him merited that he would be saved. Unfortunately, the opposite occurred. God criticized him for his overzealous behavior. Listening to the divine criticism, Elijah remembered that God blamed Moses for zealously disparaging the Israelites. Elijah understood that both he and Moses should have spoken softly to the people to persuade them to accept the divine laws. Zealotry destroys character. God spoke with a soft voice, not as a loud, harsh windstorm, a noisy earthquake, or a burning fire. Elijah understood that God was showing Moses he was no longer an effective leader, and God ended Moses' leadership of the Israelites and killed him. As he thought of Moses, Elijah realized how wrong he had been acting, that he would also soon die, and needed to appoint a successor, as Moses did.

WHO WAS ELISHA?

Elisha was a man of wealth, as indicated by his needing to plow a large estate with twelve carts pulled by twenty-four oxen. He gave up his secure life to serve Elijah. Our introduction to him shows him to have a different personality than Elijah. Unlike Elijah, who was over-zealous for God and ignored people's feelings, Elisha's first concern was for his parents and the needs of the people he employed. He displayed the character traits that God wanted Elijah to show. God does not need or want over-zealousness directed to heaven but kindness to people on earth.

However, this introduction to Elisha changes. We learn of his faults. He accompanies Elijah when Elijah goes to die. He engages, as we will see in three activities showing arrogance. He also tells people to do things that make no sense.

OBSCURITIES IN THE ELISHA NARRATIVES

Readers need to be alert that the stories of Elisha are filled with obscurities. Commentators frequently differ in how they interpret what they read. Often, one will criticize while the other will praise. The two main events in the first chapter serve as examples. Why was Elisha, seemingly a friendly man, attracted to the wild, individualistic, zealous Elijah? Was Elisha always a friendly man? Why did he want to serve, be a disciple, or successor to Elijah? Was he conflicted? Did he see Elijah as the ideal human?

Secondly, readers should remember that Maimonides wrote in the second book of his *Guide for the Perplexed*, chapter 48, that whenever the Bible states that God said or did something, God did not do it. The event occurred according to natural law. God is credited for the action only because God created or formed natural law. According to Maimonides, neither Elijah's nor Elisha's behaviors involved God. What did the author or authors of the stories of Elijah and Elisha want readers to think? Did they approve of their statements and actions?

There are many other obscurities in the narratives. Each is designed to encourage us to think and learn to act according to the Golden Rule of loving all as one loves oneself and wants to be treated. In this chapter, for example, we have no idea why twelve teams of oxen are mentioned. Do they symbolize the twelve tribes? But Elijah and Elisha lived among the ten tribes. Does the number indicate the view of the author or authors that God is the God of all the tribes, and prophets must stress this to the people? How should we understand the number 7,000? Is it also symbolic? Does it use the frequently appearing number seven to tell us something? Does the word "thousand" indicate a group?

THREE FINAL COMMANDS TO ELIJAH

God tells Elijah to anoint Hazael king over Aram and Jehu king over Israel. God also told Elijah to annoint Elisha as his replacement. It is inconceivable that Elijah was able to anoint a non-Israelite king and anoint a king over Israel two decades after his death. The first two assignments should be taken with a grain of salt. God is telling Elijah, or using his intelligence, Elijah realizes that Ahab's dynasty will be destroyed. Hazael will punish the Israelites in a war,[2] Jehu with a

---

2.   II Kings 8.

rebellion against Ahab's descendant,[3] and Elijah is rebuked for his overzealousness.[4] Malbim states that the three persons mentioned correspond to Elijah's three critiques about the Israelites in verses 10 and 14.[5] We may think of other interpretations.

WHY DID ELIJAH REBUKE ELISHA?

Elisha agreed to follow Elijah instantly but requested permission to say farewell to his parents. Elijah responded, "Go on back, for what have I done to you?"

We need to clarify what he meant. Was Elijah testing Elisha as God tested him at Sinai, also called Horeb? Is Elisha firm in deciding to face the idolatrous Israelites? Or is Elijah saying, I haven't even hinted that you should not take the time to say farewell to your parents?

Elisha took more time than saying farewell to his parents before leaving with Elijah. He killed the two oxen that pulled his cart, prepared them for a meal, and served them as food for many people. Rashi suggests that he acted out of great joy in being able to be Elijah's servant. His act in thinking about the needs of people who had suffered hunger because of the drought contrasts markedly with Elijah's zealousness toward God while ignoring the needs of the human population. But Rashi suggests that Elisha was impetuous. This is a character trait we will see later. He was in such a hurry to accompany Elijah that he did not take the time to search for wood but broke up his cart and used the wood to make a fire to prepare the food. However, Ehrlich chides Rashi for missing the point. Elisha, who had until now engaged in the work of the general population, realized that, henceforth, he would have a higher calling. So, as a sign to himself and others, he killed the oxen with which he plowed his field and destroyed the cart they pulled to demonstrate that this was no longer his work. Ehrlich also suggests that the kindhearted Elisha invited Elijah, who had not eaten nor drunk for forty days, to partake in the food.

The contrasting methodologies of Rashi and Ehrlich show why I generally enjoy Ehrilch's manner of interpreting scripture.

---

3. II Kings 9.

4. Adin Steinsaltz, *HaTanakh HaMevoar: Hamesh Megillot*, with Commentary (Jerusalem: Koren Press, 2017).

5. Malbim (Meir Leibush ben Yehiel Michel Wisser), *Otzar Haperushim al Nakh, Mefarshei Hatanakh*, undated.

Chapter 2

ELISHA ASSUMES ELIJAH'S ROLE

I Kings 20 to 22 and II Kings 1 deal with Ahab. They interrupt the narrative about Elijah. Elijah's story continues from I Kings 19 to II Kings 2. Chapter two has three of the twenty-nine Elisha activities. He parts the Jordan just as Elijah did. Moses did the same at Marah in Exodus 15:23-25. Then, he aids people by healing harmful waters. We do not know how the water is contaminated. We also have no idea how casting salt into the water cured it. This could be simply a magician's sleight of hand. He distracted the onlookers with the salt and did something else. The text is obscure. Then, he murdered forty-two children, which is inconceivable and seemingly improper.

II KINGS CHAPTER 2

1. It happened that Elijah went with Elisha from Gilgal when the Lord would take up Elijah by a whirlwind to heaven.

2. Elijah told Elisha, "Please wait here, for *Y-H-V-H* sent me to Beth-el." Elisha responded, "As *Y-H-V-H* lives, and as you live, I will not leave you." So, they went down to Beth-el.

3. The budding prophets [literally, "sons of the prophets"]¹ who were at Beth-el came to Elisha and said to him, "Do you know that *Y-H-V-H* will

---

1. There are five mentions of *bnei hanevi'im* in II Kings, in 2:2, 2:5, 2:15, 4:1, and 6:1. The term means "sons of the prophets." It is somewhat similar to *bnei Yisrael*, "sons of Israel," which should be translated into English as Israelites. But there are two differences. The one referring to prophets adds the Hebrew letter *hay*, meaning "the." Also, while all the people were Israelites, the stories of the budding prophets depict them as individuals hoping to reach Elisha's level of prophecy, but not yet doing so. Therefore, I suggest the translation "budding prophets."

take away your master from your head today?" He said, "Yes, I also know it. Be silent."

4. Elijah said to him, "Elisha, please wait here, for *Y-H-V-H* sent me to Jericho." He answered, "As *Y-H-V-H* lives, and as you live, I will not leave you." So, they came to Jericho.

5. The budding prophets at Jericho came to Elisha and said to him, "Do you know that *Y-H-V-H* will take away your master from your head today?" He answered, "Yes, I also know it. Be silent."

6. Elijah said to him, "Please wait here, for the Lord has sent me to the Jordan." He said, "As the Lord lives, and as you live, I will not leave you." The two went on.

7. Fifty men of the budding prophets went and stood facing from afar. Two of them stood by the Jordan.[2]

8. Elijah wrapped his mantle together, struck the waters, and divided them here and there so the two went over on dry ground.

9. When they went over, Elijah instructed Elisha, "Ask what I should do for you before I am taken from you." Elisha responded, "Let me have a double portion of your spirit."

10. He said, "You requested a difficult thing. Nevertheless, if you see me when I am taken from you, you will have it, but if not, it will not happen."

11. As they continued walking and talking, a chariot of fire appeared with horses of fire that parted the two of them, and Elijah ascended in a whirlwind to heaven.

12. Elisha saw it and cried, "My father, my father,[3] [the] chariot of Israel and its horsemen!"[4] He saw him no more. He took hold of his clothes and tore them in two pieces.

13. He also took up the mantle of Elijah that fell from him and went back and stood by the bank of the Jordan.

---

2. Some scholars ponder whether there is any relationship between these fifty sons of the prophets and the fifty that Obadiah hid in two caves, fifty each, but are unable to resolve this question.

3. Students are called "children," and teachers "fathers" because teachers give birth to ideas to their pupils (Gersonides). Catholics may like to be called "father" because of this idea.

4. The Aramaic Targum has, "My master, my master, who did better for Israel by his prayers than chariots and horsemen."

14. He took the mantle of Elijah that fell from him, struck the waters, and said, "Where is the Lord, the God of Elijah?"[5] He hit the water. It divided here and there. And Elisha went over.

15. Some distance away, the budding prophets at Jericho said, "The spirit of Elijah rests on Elisha." They came to meet him and bowed on the ground before him.[6]

16. They told him, "Your servants are fifty strong men. Please let them go and seek your master. Perhaps the Lord's spirit lifted and cast him on some mountain or valley." He said, "Do not go."

17. When they urged him until he was ashamed, he said, "Go." Fifty men searched for him for three days. They did not find him.

18. They returned while he was still in Jericho. He said to them, "Didn't I tell you not to go?"

19. The city men said to Elisha, "Note, please, the city's situation is pleasant as my lord sees. But the water is terrible, and the land miscarries."

20. He said, "Bring me a new cruse and place salt in it." They brought it to him.

21. He went to the source of the water and tossed the salt in it. He said, "This is what Y-H-V-H said, 'I have healed these waters. There will be no more deaths nor miscarrying from it.'"

22. So the waters were healed until today, as Elisha said.

23. He went from there to Beth-el. While on the way, young city children came from the city and mocked him. They said, "Go away baldy, go away baldy."

24. He looked back, saw them, and cursed them using the name Y-H-V-H. So, two female bears came from the woods and tore forty-two of the children.

25. He went from there to Mount Carmel and from there to Samaria.

HOW SHOULD WE UNDERSTAND VERSES 9 AND 12?

Verse 9 contains a conversation where Elisha requests that Elijah give him twice his powers. When they went over the Jordan, Elijah instructed Elisha, "Ask what I should do for you before I am taken from you." Elisha responded, "Let me have

---

5.   Elisha is not questioning the existence of God. He is invoking the power of God, as if he is saying, now show the divine power. The Aramaic Targum treats it as a prayer: "accept my prayer, Lord God of Elijah." Steinsaltz interprets Elisha saying, Elijah is no longer here, but God is here.

6.   They bowed to Elisha as Obadiah respectfully bowed to Elijah in 18:7.

a double portion of your spirit." The author or authors of Kings may be relating two things to readers. The first is negative. Despite Elisha having much respect for Elijah and being willing to leave his present life to be his successor, he needs to think of himself as a superior person and is unafraid of expressing his feelings. This is the first of many occasions where he acts abruptly with others because they are not treating him as he feels they should. We will see this in verses 23 and 24. Elisha was brilliant and essentially a good man. But like all of us, he is human. He has faults. The Hebrew Bible makes it clear that there is no human without faults. The rabbis revealed faults in every patriarch, even our teacher Moses, who insulted the Israelites because of his love of God when they demanded water. Even King David, whom tradition tells us is the progenitor of the Messiah, committed adultery and killed the husband of the woman he bedded. By revealing the human faults of superior people, scripture reminds us that despite our mistakes, we can excel. The second possible interpretation is positive. The text foretells that Elisha will exceed the number of helpful deeds Elijah performed.[7]

In verse 12, Elisha shouts, "My father, my father, [the] chariot of Israel and its horsemen!" Later, in chapter 13, the king of Israel applies these words to Elisha while he is dying. The second usage by the king is understandable. The king referred to Israel's enemy country, Moab, which had many war chariots and a large military force, while Israel lacked these physical instruments. Yet, Elisha was a better chariot and horseman than Israel's foe. His advice to Israel during his more than sixty years allowed Israel to defeat Moab. However, the title is inappropriate for Elijah, who never helped the king of Israel defeat enemy forces. Elijah, in contrast, restricted his activities to zealously trying to persuade Israelites to abandon idol worship and cling to God. We can understand that Elisha applied his own goal to Elijah because he respected him, even though Elijah did not live up to his compliment.

HOW SHOULD WE UNDERSTAND VERSES 23 AND 24?
The two biblical books of Kings generally exaggerate numbers. They use 50 or a multiple of it, such as 450 pagan priests, 100 prophets, and 50 budding prophets. Here, 42 is used. This number is precise. It calls attention to itself. Like verse 12, the text alerts us that although Elisha was brilliant and performed many helpful

---

7. In contrast, *Olam Hatanakh*, Divrei Hayamim, Melachim Bet, suggests the text does not mean double but two thirds.

acts for Israel, he, like all humans, had faults and made mistakes. This is one of them. Unfortunately, not the last.

The tale of the mocking children and the bears is troubling. A rabbi in the Babylonian Talmud *Sotah* 46b tries to weaken the problem of an overreaction by not defining the Hebrew *ne'arim* as children but as irreligious youths. F.J. Foakes-Jackson reduces the severity of criticism against Elisha in *The Biblical History of the Hebrews*,[8] by pointing out that the text does not say the youths were killed. They may have only been wounded.

It is also possible that the rascals were not mocking baldness, a natural male phenomenon, but belittling Elisha for assuming Elijah's prophetic role by comparing the two. Elijah was hairy, as stated in II Kings 1:8. But Elisha looked nothing like him. He was bald.

WHY DID ELIJAH INSTRUCT ELISHA TO REMAIN WHERE HE WAS?

Elijah tells Elisha three times that he is going somewhere and that Elisha should not accompany him. First to Beth-el. Then, perhaps after reaching this city, Jericho. Then the Jordan. Why is he going to each town? Why doesn't he want Elisha to accompany him? We don't know. Slotki states that some commentators said Elijah was modest and did not want Elisha to see God take him to heaven. He also suggests that children of prophets were in each city, and Elijah wanted to bid them farewell.

The latter is reasonable, but the former idea is less so. There would be no miracle. Elijah realized he was dying and wanted to die at the Jordan for an unknown reason. But he did not wish Elisha to see him die. The trip to the Jordan went through Beth-el and Jericho. Before each city, he tried unsuccessfully to persuade Elisha to wait behind.

It is also likely that this book's author or authors wanted to compare Elijah's death to that of Moses and show that Elijah was no Moses. Moses died alone. Elijah also wished to die alone but failed to do so.

The book compares Elijah to Moses and Joshua, highlighting similarities and differences. All three divided water using some item, but Moses and Joshua divided the water with a rod, and Elijah and Elisha did so with Elijah's mantle. We do not know the significance of the difference.

---

8.   F.J. Foakes-Jackson, *The Biblical History of the Hebrews* (Legare Street Press, 2023).

Ehrlich writes that God did not send Elijah to any of these three places; Elijah was testing Elisha to see if he would accompany him. Malbim supposes that Elisha did not want to leave Elijah because he didn't want to lose the opportunity to request Elijah to give him a double portion.[9]

THE SPLITTING OF THE JORDAN

Counting Joshua's splitting the Jordan, Jordan's splitting occurred three times. Additionally, Moses split the Red Sea.

There is probably no significance in that Moses hit a rock, a solid object in Exodus 17:1–17 and Numbers 20:1–13 from which came water, while here Elijah and Elisha struck the water, resulting in dry solid land; but it is an interesting contrast.

It is unclear why Elijah had to cross the Jordan and be outside the jurisdiction of Israel when he ascended in the chariot (died). It is conceivable that the book is making another comparison between Elijah and Moses. The two died on the east side of the Jordan after transferring leadership to their successor. Radak reflects this idea. He writes that Elijah and Elisha went toward the mountain Moses ascended before he died.

Verse 14 needs clarification. It states that Elisha hit the water, prayed, then hit it again, and the Jordan split after the second strike. There is no explanation for why Elisha needed to hit the water twice and why he had to pray before the second hit. This baffled many translators and commentators, such as Gersonides, who hid the problem by translating, "*When* he had struck the waters," indicating that Elisha struck the water only once. The author or authors of Kings may again be comparing Elijah to Moses, reminding readers that Moses struck a rock twice in Exodus 17 and Numbers 20 to produce water.

Malbim supposes that Elijah had the power to split the Jordan only because Elisha was with him; the "miracle" needed their combined holiness. When Elisha tried to break the Jordan alone, he could not do so until he reminded God that Elijah had given him a double portion, which Malbim understood as the power of Elijah being added to his ability. Now that he had the strength of both, he could divide the Jordan.

---

9. Verse 9.

WHO WERE THE SONS OF THE PROPHETS, AND WHAT WERE THEY TELLING ELISHA?

We do not know who these people were. The Aramaic Targum translates "sons" as "students," prophets in training, or regular students learning about Judaism and secular studies. Abarbanel proposes that they were students learning how to prophesy. They may have been the sons of the prophets that Jezebel killed. Radak supposes that the sons of the prophets were capable of predicting, but only about current events, not the future. Therefore, what they said was not written and saved for posterity. They, like Elisha, were able to see that Elijah was dying. They mentioned this to Elisha. He told them he also knew it, and it was best to be silent about it.

Cogan and Tadmor explain that *ben* indicates a member of a guild, order, or class. They are a loosely organized group living together in towns in northern Israel. They are not the same kind of people as the "band of prophets" in I Samuel 10:5 and 19:20–24.[10]

Kiel observes that since the sons of the prophets were now able, in contrast to chapter 18, to appear openly without fear of Jezebel, it shows that Jezebel had ceased killing prophets of the Lord.[11]

There are three appearances of the sons of the prophets before Elijah's death, twice warning Elisha what they saw about Elijah and once as they stood at a distance and saw Elisha become Elijah's successor. Scripture and other cultures use "three" often.

WHAT WAS THE DOUBLE PORTION OF SPIRIT THAT ELISHA REQUESTED OF ELIJAH?

We do not know. It may be related to the double portion in Deuteronomy 21:17 that a father should give to his firstborn, while other children receive only a single part of an inheritance. Or, it may be a metaphor. Elisha was requesting that Elijah identify him as Elijah's successor. J. Robinson sees Elisha saying, "Treat me as a firstborn son."[12]

---

10. Mordechai Cogan and Hayim Tadmor, *II Kings*, The Anchor Bible (Doubleday & Company, Inc, 1988).

11. Y. Kiel, *Sefer Melachim*, volume two (Jerusalem: Mossad Harav Kook, 1989).

12. J. Robinson, *The Second Book of Kings*, The Cambridge Bible Commentary Series (Cambridge University Press, 1976).

When Elijah tells him that if he sees Elijah pass away, "you will have it," he tells him that Elisha will see what to do to be accepted as Elijah's successor. Elisha did so. "He took up the mantle of Elijah that fell off him." Malbim's view is mentioned previously. Kiel notes that many rabbis understood Elisha's request literally: he wanted twice Elijah's power, and these rabbis say Elisha received twice Elijah's power; he performed twice as many miracles as Elijah.

Chapter 3

ELISHA AIDS THE KINGS OF ISRAEL AND JUDAH

Chapter three has three of the twenty-nine Elisha activities. He performs his first act for the sake of the nation of Israel. He insults Israel's king and the king's parents. Then prophesizes that a valley will be filled with water. He follows it with a prophecy that the Moabites would think the water was filled with Israel's blood. The two prophecies raise problems for us. But first, some background.

II KINGS CHAPTER 3

11. Jehoshaphat [the king of Judah] asked, "Isn't there a prophet of *Y-H-V-H* here from whom we could enquire of *Y-H-V-H*?" One of the king of Israel's servants replied. He said, "Elisha the son of Shaphat is here. He poured water on the hands of Elijah."

12. Jehoshaphat said, "He has *Y-H-V-H*'s word." So the king of Israel, Jehoshaphat, and the king of Edom went down to him.

13. Elisha said to the king of Israel, "What have I to do with you? Go to the prophets of your father and the prophets of your mother." The king of Israel said to him, "No. Because *Y-H-V-H* summoned these three kings to deliver them into the hand of Moab."

14. Elisha said, "As *Y-H-V-H* of hosts lives, whom I stand before, were it not because of the presence of Jehoshaphat the king of Judah, I would not look at you or see you.

15. But now bring me a minstrel." When the minstrel played, the hand of Y-H-V-H came upon him.

16. And he said, "*Y-H-V-H* said this, 'Fill this valley with ditches.'"

17. *Y-H-V-H* said, "You will not see wind nor rain. Yet this valley will be filled with water. You will drink, you, your cattle, and your beasts.

18. This is a light thing in the *Y-H-V-H*'s sight. He will [also] deliver the Moabites into your hand.

19. You will smite every fortified city and every choice city, topple every good tree, stop all water wells, and mar every good piece of land with stones."

20. It happened in the morning when the offering was offered that water came from Edom, and the country was filled with water.

21. When all the Moabites heard that the kings came up to fight them, they gathered everyone who could wear armor and upward and stood at the border.

22. They rose early in the morning. The sun shined on the water, and the Moabites saw the water in the distance as red as blood:

23. They exclaimed, "This is blood. The kings are surely slain. They killed one another. Now Moab, to the spoil!"

24. The Israelites rose and smote when they arrived at the Israelite camp. They smote the Moabites so that they fled before them. So Israel smote the land of Moab.

25. They beat down the cities. Every man cast his stone on every good piece of land and filled it. They stopped all the wells of water and felled all the good trees. They left stones only in Kirharaseth. And slingers went about it and smote it.

26. When the king of Moab saw that the battle was lost, he assembled seven hundred men who drew swords to break through to the king of Edom, but they failed.

27. Then he took his eldest son, who should have reigned in his stead, and offered him as a burnt offering upon the wall. And there was great indignation against Israel. They departed from him and returned to their land.

A PROBLEM

Ever since the time of Solomon's son, the tribes have been divided into two kingdoms. Judah was in the south with remnants of the tribe of Shimon. The ten other tribes called themselves Israel and were in the north. Often, the two did not get along. Often, as in the time of Elisha, the ten were idol worshippers. Elisha sided with Judah, who worshiped the true God during his time.

Chapter three began when the northern and southern kings decided to work with the king of Edom because they feared a Moabite attack. The king of Judah wanted help from Elisha.

Elisha welcomed them but said he would not have even looked at the king of Israel if the king of Judah, whom he respected, had not requested his help. It is this harsh statement to a king that raises one problem.

In the former chapters, we saw how Elisha acted toward other people. He requested that Elijah hand him powers that exceeded those Elijah had. He was critical of the sons of the prophets who wanted to check if Elijah's body could be found. He caused two bears to harm youths who harassed him. Rabbis and secular scholars had difficulty suggesting how to understand that Elisha acted reasonably. Now, we hear him insulting a king and the king's parents. People criticize their rulers in writing or on TV today, but isn't it arrogance to do so to their face?

Is Elisha showing arrogance? Is he behaving as a zealot, sure his way is correct, and others can be ignored and insulted? Is he oblivious to the Golden Rule to love others as you love yourself? Is he copying Elijah, whom God killed for this behavior? The beginning of Elijah's and Elisha's name is *El*, which means God. Both love God. But is their approach to God overly zealous? Is it possible that God did not advise Elijah to pick Elisha as his successor, but Elijah selected a man with his views and behaviors?

ANOTHER SERIOUS PROBLEM

In the prior chapters, Elisha performed three significant acts, which could be called miracles. He split the Jordan. He cured foul water. He caused scoundrels who harassed him to be harmed. Each of these events is somewhat understandable. But the details are obscure. We do not know why they are stated. We do not even know if they are miracles. The text does not say so but implies it. This happens frequently in the Book of Kings.

For example. Elisha tells people to get him a cruse and salt. Commentators say they are symbols. But do not say they caused the foul water to become pure. How did Elisha purify the water? How did he do the other activities? How should readers of the stories understand these details? No commentator enlightens us on how Elisha accomplished his acts. Is it possible that the author or authors of these narratives is mocking us? Are they saying Elisha's acts are like the tricks of modern magicians? The trickster says, watch my hand, look at the cruse, don't take your eyes off the salt. Then, unobserved, he performs his trick.

In his *Guide for the Perplexed*, Maimonides informed us that prophecy is the thinking of humans with advanced intelligence and understanding. Each prophet needed an excellent imagination to place his ideas in a manner people could understand. Since people have different levels of intelligence and imagination, the prophecies of each prophet are presented in different ways. How are Elisha's prophecies different?

OTHER INTERPRETATIONS OF THE CHAPTER

The Judean king Jehoshaphat suggested to Jehoram, king of Israel, to enquire of Elisha because he felt seeking advice from idol-worshipping priests was a waste of time. Besides, he thought Elisha could assure him that Jehoram's fear was justified. He did not want to go to war unless it was necessary. He knew nothing about Elisha. This was why he had to ask if there was a prophet of Y-H-V-H in the Israel kingdom. Jehoram's servant suggested Elisha and said he poured water on Elijah's hands. Jehoshaphat knew about Elijah, as shown by his acceptance of the suggestion. The metaphor about the water describes an intimate, devoted connection of Elisha to Elijah.

Elisha requests a minstrel appear to play music to inspire him, as in I Samuel 10:5. It is also possible that he wanted the music to calm him so that he could think. He wasn't accustomed to appearing before kings. When inspired or relaxed, he ordered the digging of trenches, which would miraculously be filled with water. This instruction is an example of Elisha's obscure requests. Yes, water came. But Elisha does not predict that the Moabite king would be deceived by the sun's reddish reflection in the water to think his enemies fought among themselves and killed one another.

Elisha instructs the three kings to destroy everything belonging to Moab, even fruit-bearing trees. This is a surprising violation of Deuteronomy 20:19, where the act is forbidden. Why did he say this? Was he carried away, over-enthusiastic?

Verse 24 has the word *vayabo* (and they came). The Masorites corrected it to *vayaku* (they smote). The correction results in "smote" appearing three times, indicating a decisive outcome.

The chapter's final verse is unclear. Commentators debate who killed whom. Was it the king of Moab who sacrificed his son as an offering to his god, hoping the god would save him? Or, are the commentators who say the Moabite king murdered the son of his rival, the king of Edom, whom the Moabite king held as a captive correct? He murdered him as revenge for the Edomite king's alliance with Israel and Judah against him.

The final sentence of the chapter has another obscurity, "*And there was great indignation against Israel. They departed from him and returned to their land*" is inexplicable. We have no idea who was angry against whom or why and who returned home.

Chapter 4

ELISHA AIDS FOUR: TWO WOMEN, SONS OF PROPHETS, AND A MAN

This chapter has five Elisha activities. All show the prophet doing helpful acts. Elisha does not insert something to accomplish his miracle in three activities. They appear to be miracles, but they may be natural occurrences, although how they are done is obscure. In one of the five, Elisha caused vessels to be filled with oil. In another, he prophesied a Shunammite woman would have a son. The third shows him resurrecting this son. In the fourth, he casts meal into a pot where there was "harm." It is unclear whether the harm means poison or a bitter taste. It is also uncertain how the inserted meal changed the situation. We can also compare this deed to that of Moses in the wilderness when the people cried that their water was bitter, and Moses tossed an object into it and cured the problem. Elisha's fifth act causes scant bread to feed a hundred men.

II KINGS CHAPTER 4

1. A certain woman of the wives of the budding prophets cried to Elisha, saying, "Your servant, my husband, is dead. You know that your servant feared Y-H-V-H. The creditor came to take my two sons to be bondmen."
2. Elisha said to her, "What should I do for you? Tell me what you have in the house." She answered, "Your handmaid has nothing in the house except a pot of oil."
3. He said, "Go, borrow vessels from all your neighbors, empty containers; borrow more than a few.
4. When you return, shut the door before you and your sons, and pour out [from your pot of oil] into all those vessels. Then, set aside the packed jars."

5. She left him, shut the door before her and her sons, those who brought the vessels to her, and poured out.

6. When the vessels were full, she told a son, "Bring me more vessels." He responded to her, "There are no more vessels." And the oil stayed.

7. She came and told this to the man of God. He said, "Go, sell the oil, pay your debt, and you and your sons live on the rest."

8. It happened one day that Elisha passed to Shunem. There was a great woman there. She persuaded him to eat bread. So, whenever he passed by, he turned there to eat bread.

9. She told her husband, "Now I see that he who passes by us frequently is a holy man of God.

10. Please let's make a small chamber on the roof, set a bed there for him, a table, a chair, and a candlestick so he could go there when he comes to us."

11. A day came when he arrived. He went to the upper chamber and lay there.

12. He said to Gehazi, his servant, "Call this Shunammite." When he called her, she stood before him.

13. He told him, "Please tell her, You treated us well with all this care. What can be done for you? Would you [prefer that I] speak for you to the king or the military chief?" She answered, "I dwell among my people."

14. So he asked, "What can be done for her?" Gehazi said, "Unfortunately, she has no child, and her husband is old."

15. He said, "Call her." He called her, and she stood in the door.

16. He said, "At this time, when [all life] is reviving, you will embrace a son." She responded, "No, my lord, man of God, do not lie to your handmaid."

17. The woman conceived. She bore a son at that time, when there was reviving, just as Elisha said.

18. The child grew. One day, he went to his father to the reapers.

19. He cried to his father, "My head, my head." He said to a lad, "Carry him to his mother."

20. He took him to his mother. He sat on her knees until noon and then died.

21. She went up, laid him on the bed of the man of God, shut the door before him, and went out.

22. She called her husband and said, "Please send me one of the servants and one of the asses so that I could run to the man of God and return."

23. He asked, "Why do you go to him today? It is neither new moon nor Sabbath?" She responded, "All will be well."

24. She saddled an ass and said to her servant, "Drive, go forward. Do not reduce the pace except when I tell you."

25. So she went and came to the man of God to Mount Carmel. When the man of God saw her from a distance, he said to Gehazi, his servant, "There is the Shunammite.

26. Please run now to meet her and ask, 'Is it well with you? Is it well with your husband? Is it well with the child?'" She replied, "It is well."

27. When she came to the man of God to the hill, she caught hold of his feet. Gehazi came near to thrust her away. But the man of God said, "Let her alone. She is in pain. Y-H-V-H hid it from me and did not tell me".

28. Then she said, "Did I request a son of my lord? Didn't I say, Do not deceive me?"

29. Then he said to Gehazi, "Go fast. Take hold of my staff, and go. If you meet any man, don't greet him. If he greets you, don't respond. Lay my staff on the child's face."

30. The child's mother said, "As Y-H-V-H lives, and as you live, I will not leave you." He arose and followed her.

31. Gehazi went before them. He laid the staff on the child's face. But there was neither voice nor hearing. He returned to meet him. He told him, "The child has not awakened."

32. So when Elisha came into the house, the child was dead, lying on his bed.

33. He went in, shut the door before the two of them, and prayed to Y-H-V-H.

34. Then he went, laid on the child, put his mouth on his mouth, his eyes on his eyes, his hands on his hands, stretched himself over the child, and the child's flesh became warm.

35. Then he left [the bed] and walked in the house to and fro. Then he went up and stretched himself upon him. The child sneezed seven times, and the child opened his eyes.

36. He called Gehazi and said, "Call the Shunammite." He called her. When she came to him, he said, "Take your son."

37. She entered, fell at his feet, bowed to the ground, took up her son, and left.

38. Then Elisha returned to Gilgal. There was a famine in the land. The budding prophets were sitting before him. He instructed his servant, "Set up the great pot and boil pottage for the budding prophets."

39. Someone went to the field to gather herbs and found a wild vine. He picked a lap full of wild fruit from it, came, and shredded them into the pot of pottage, although they knew nothing about the product.

40. They poured it out for the men to eat. While eating the pottage, they cried and said, "Man of God, there is death in the pot." And they could not eat it.

41. But he said, "Then bring meal." He cast it into the pot and said, "Pour it out for the people to eat. There no harm in the pot."

42. There came a man from Baal-shalishah. He brought the man of God bread of the first fruits, twenty loaves of barley, and full ears of corn in the husk. And he said, "Give it to the people to eat."

43. His servant said, "What, should I set this before a hundred men?" He repeated, "Give it to the people, for *Y-H-V-H* said, 'They will eat and leave some.'"

44. So he set it before them, they ate, and left some. As *Y-H-V-H* said.

SOME INTERPRETATIONS OF THE CHAPTER

The first two episodes involve unnamed women. Why? According to Jewish tradition, the first woman was the wife of Obadiah, Ahab's servant mentioned in I Kings 18:3ff. This tradition identifies the creditor as Jehoram, Ahab's son. He lent money to Obadiah, who needed the funds to maintain the prophets hiding from Ahab. Elisha advised the woman to shut the door to avoid publicity. The words "the oil stayed" means the oil ceased increasing. Unlike his prior activities, this incident with the oil has no obscure details. But we have no idea how Elisha caused the oil to increase.

The second episode focuses on a woman living in Shunem. She is called a Shunammite. Like the former woman, she is not named. We do not know if the author or authors ignored naming them because they demeaned women. According to Jewish tradition, this second woman was the sister of Abishag, the Shunammite mentioned in I Kings 1:3.[1]

---

1. The traditions for both women is in the commentary of Slotki, *Kings*, The Soncino Press, 1950.

The Shunammite woman did not realize at first that Elisha was a prophet. Yet, she was hospitable. She built a room for him and arranged basic, comfortable essentials. When he offers to repay her by using his influence with the king and the military, she responds that she does not need outside help because her relatives can aid her. Gehazi suggests that she cannot have a child because her husband is old, and Elisha can petition God to cause her to have a child.

While verse 20 states the child died, we cannot be sure this is true. It is more likely that the child only appeared to be so. This understanding is supported by seeing Elisha's acts as measures to restore breathing, artificial respiration. Why she did not reveal the youth's apparent death to her husband and later to Elisha's servant is unclear. She may have wanted to rush to the prophet for help and not pause for seconds to give explanations.

Elisha's prediction of the birth of a child to a childless woman parallels the tales in Genesis 18:9–15, Judges 13:2–5, and I Samuel 1:17, as well as a version of the birth of Jesus in the New Testament. The seemingly unnatural feeding of many hungry people also parallels Exodus 16, Numbers 11, and an act by Jesus in the New Testament.

A DIGEST OF JUDAISM

II Kings 4 describes a troubled woman who discovers her son has died. She rushes to leave her home and seeks Elisha's help. Her husband did not know his son died. He asks her in verse 23, "Why do you go to him today? It is neither new moon nor Sabbath?" The chapter does not explain the husband's words. They reflect some Jewish practices.

In Exodus 33, Moses requests God to reveal what He is. God replies that humans cannot understand anything about Him other than what they can learn by studying what He created or formed. Later, in Deuteronomy 32:1, Moses repeats this insight when he calls heaven and earth as two witnesses to testify metaphorically to the existence of God, His laws, and that people will benefit by performing these laws.

Judaism does not require Jews to believe anything or have faith. It requires Jews to act, to do what God wants them to do. The Hebrew word *emunah*, translated in Modern Hebrew as belief and faith, refers to actions in the Bible. When I was a youngster, my father, the brilliant Rabbi Dr. Nathan Drazin, took me to a lecture by the famous Rabbi Abraham Joshua Heschel (1907–1972). Rabbi

Heschel explained that the biblical *emunah* does not mean "faith" but being "faithful" in actions. I was so impressed that I requested my father to take me to the podium to meet the rabbi. When he did, I asked the rabbi to sell me his book and autograph it. He did. Although more than seventy years have passed since I met him, I never forgot his insight.

Moses taught this lesson to the Israelites during the last days of his life. He uses many words, each emphasizing action. He repeats his message many times because of its importance. For example, when he recalls the Decalogue announced at Mount Sinai, he changes Exodus 20's "Remember the Sabbath Day," focusing on thinking, to "Observe the Sabbath Day," requiring an act.

When I left home at age twenty-one to serve in the US Army, my father echoed the teachings of Moses. My father's advice to me was, "Israel, be sure to observe Shabbat. More than you keeping Shabbat, Shabbat will keep you." Thinking is undoubtedly important. But acts produce results.

The seventh day Sabbath is so significant that Jews repeat the number seven in over a hundred different Jewish observances to remind us of Shabbat's impact on observers.

In biblical times, the ancient practice concerning the new moon was to refrain from work and bring special sacrifices, as indicated in Numbers 28:1–15 and elsewhere. In I Samuel 20:5, the new moon also became when people gathered for a festive meal. Later, in the time of Elisha, people also visited wise men to learn from them.

One of the many ways that Jews used seven was the seventh new moon. This is similar to how Jewish ancestors marked the seventh week as the holiday Shavuot, the seventh year was Shemita, the seventh Shemita was the jubilee year, etc. The seventh new moon was called "The Day of the Blowing of a Trumpet" in Numbers 29:1 and "The Day of Recalling Events by the Blowing of a Trumpet" in Leviticus 23:23–25.

I am writing this on September 11, 2023, the day Americans recall the 9/11 tragedies when over 3,000 people were murdered by terrorists in the attack that destroyed the Twin Towers in New York. Bugles are blown with taps in many localities to remember, just as trumpets on "The Day of Recalling Events by the Blowing of a Trumpet."

The husband of the distraught woman whose son died, who knew nothing of the death, could not understand why his wife wanted to rush to the prophet.

While the ancient practice was to visit wise men on Shabbat and holidays to learn from them, the day she was running was neither.

When the Romans destroyed Israel and its Temple in 70 CE, Judaism changed in many ways. Leaders of the Pharisees began to be called rabbis. Earlier great sages such as Hillel and Shammai did not have this title. Clerics who claim Jesus was a rabbi are wrong. The title did not exist when he is said to have lived from about 4 BCE to about 25 CE.[2] Since Sacrifices that could only be offered in the Temple ceased, some holidays, such as Passover on 14 Nisan, which depended only on sacrifices, stopped. Its name was given to The Festival of Matzot, which started on 15 Nisan.

So, too, "The Day of Recalling Events by the Blowing of a Trumpet," when sacrifices were brought, was replaced by Rosh Hashanah, a non-biblical holiday. The blowing of a shofar continued, as did the idea of remembrance. But now, the recollections focus on past behaviors and how to improve them.[3]

WHAT DOES "MAN OF GOD" MEAN?

The biblical book Kings describes the Deity as Y-H-V-H, as did the Five Books of Moses. It also calls the Deity Elohim, generally translated as "God," as does the Five Books. Yet, it describes the prophet Elisha as a "Man of Elohim," not a "Man of Y-H-V-H." Why?

A related question. Are the many secular scholars correct when they claim that the biblical sections that mention Elohim and Y-H-V-H were written by different authors?

A third question. How should we understand the introduction to the Five Books of Moses?

It should be clear that secular scholars would agree that there is no conflict of writers in the story of Elisha, with some giving an Elohim interpretation of the tale, while, in contrast, others give another view when Y-H-V-H appears. I think the same applies to Moses' Torah.

---

2. The man who developed the calendar erred in assigning year 1 to the birth of Jesus, He forgot that the New Testament tells the tale of Herod seeking to kill him. Herod died in 4 BCE.

3. The new moon holiday is still practiced by many Jews in many ways including special prayers instead of sacrifices which are recited on these occasions.

We can see the distinction between Elohim and *Y-H-V-H* in the introductory parable of the Torah as being similar to the following. Imagine a father who has a son, Jonathan. Father sends son to the store to buy milk and says Jonathan did so. In this example, the child is described in two ways: as a son and by name.

It is the same in Genesis 1:1–2 and 2:5. The first chapter can be translated as, "In the beginning when Elohim created the heaven and earth, the earth was unformed and darkness covered all, and the wind of Elohim blew over the water." The second chapter has "*Y-H-V-H* Elohim."

Since *El* was used in ancient times to indicate something powerful, such as God, and the plural Elohim suggests something supremely powerful, there is a similarity to the use of "son" in the analogy. It describes the entity. *Y-H-V-H* is similar but more precise. It is not a name. It depicts the entity with a form of the Hebrew word meaning "being." The Being "was, is, and will be." Thus, like the analogy, we are first introduced to something (like the son in the analogy). This is something that is supremely powerful. Then, in chapter two, we are given more information. This supremely powerful entity existed forever, exists today, and will continue to exist in the future. In short, the secular scholars are wrong. There are not two ideas about God. There are two descriptions of the Deity.

Regarding the third question, how to understand the Torah's introduction, our understanding that Elohim means "very powerful" leads us to translate the verse differently than is usually proposed. Instead of "the wind of Elohim," the translation should be that "a very powerful wind blew over the water" before creation was completed.

Chapter 5

ELISHA CURES NAAMAN

Chapter five contains three of the twenty-eight Elisha activities. The first, where Elisha cures an enemy general, shows the Jewish view that people should help all people. The second contrasts the general's responses to Elisha to the criminal acts of Elisha's servant. Elisha wisely realizes that Gehazi stole items belonging to the general. The third is Elisha's effective curse punishing Gehazi.

II KINGS CHAPTER 5

1. Naaman, the military head of the king of Aram, was considered a great man by his master and held in esteem. Y-H-V-H gave victory to Aram because of him. He was a great warrior. But he was a leper.
2. The Arameans had gone in bands and brought a captive from Israel, a young woman who served Naaman's wife.
3. She suggested to her mistress, "If my lord were with the prophet in Samaria, he would heal him of his leprosy."
4. He went and told his lord, "This is what the young woman of the land of Israel said."
5. The king of Aram said, "Go. I will send a letter to the king of Israel." He left. He took ten talents of silver, six thousand pieces of gold, and ten changes of clothes.
6. He brought the letter to the king of Israel, stating, "When this letter comes to you [it will show] I sent Naaman, my servant, to you to help him recover from his leprosy."

7. When the king of Israel read the letter, he tore his clothes and said, "Am I God, to kill and to make alive, that this man sends me a man to recover from his leprosy? It seems he is seeking a quarrel with me."

8. When Elisha, the man of God, heard that the king of Israel had torn his clothes, he sent to the king, saying, "Why did you tear your clothes? Please let him come to me, and he will know there is a prophet in Israel."

9. So Naaman came with his horses and chariot and stood at the door of Elisha's house.

10. Elisha sent a messenger to him, saying, "Go and wash in the Jordan seven times, and your flesh will return to you, and you will be clean."

11. But Naaman was angry, left, and said, "I thought he would come out to me, stand, and call on the name of *Y-H-V-H* his God, wave his hand over the place, and remove the leprosy.

12. Aren't Amanah and Pharpar, rivers of Damascus, better than all the waters of Israel? Can't I wash in them and be clean?" So, he turned and departed in a rage.

13. His servants approached and said, "My father, if the prophet had suggested that you do a great thing, wouldn't you do it? So also [shouldn't you do] when he says, 'Wash and be clean'?"

14. So he went and dipped seven times in the Jordan, as the man of God said. And his flesh returned like the flesh of a little child, and he was clean.

15. He returned to the man of God, he and all his company, and stood before him. He said, "Now I know that there is no God in all the earth, but in Israel. Now, please accept a gift from your servant.

16. But he responded, "As *Y-H-V-H* lives, before whom I stand, I will receive none." He urged him to take it, but he refused.

17. Naaman said, "If so, can you please give your servant two mules' burden of earth? Your servant will in the future not offer burnt offerings or sacrifice to other gods, only to *Y-H-V-H*.

18. *Y-H-V-H* should pardon your servant for one thing. When my master goes to the house of [the god] Rimmon to worship and leans on my hand, and I bow in the house of Rimmon, [according to the practice to] bow down myself in the temple of Rimmon, *Y-H-V-H* pardon your servant for this."

19. He said unto him, "Go in peace." So, he departed from him a little way.

20. But Gehazi, Elisha the man of God's servant, thought, "My master spared Naaman the Aramean by not taking what he brought. But, as Y-H-V-H lives, I will run after him and take something from him.

21. So Gehazi followed Naaman. And when Naaman saw him running after him, he got off his chariot to meet him, and said, "Is all well?"

22. He said, "All is well. My master sent me to say, "Two young men just came to me from Mount Ephraim, budding prophets. Please give them a talent of silver and two changes of garments.

23. Naaman said, "Be content. Take two talents." He urged him, bound two silver talents in two bags, with two changes of garments, laid them on two of his servants, and they carried them before him.

24. When he came to the hill, he took them from their hand and placed them in the house. He let the men go, and they departed.

25. He went in and stood before his master. And Elisha asked him, "Where did you come from, Gehazi?" He replied, "Nowhere."

26. He said, "My heart was not with you when the man left his chariot to meet you. Is it a time to receive money, garments, olive yards, vineyards, sheep, oxen, menservants, and maidservants?

27. The leprosy of Naaman will attach itself to you and your seed forever." And he went out from his presence a leper as white as snow.

SOME COMMENTS ON THE CHAPTER

Verse 1 states that Y-H-V-H gave Aram victory. Jewish tradition identifies Naaman as the man who killed the king of Israel.[1]

The king of Aram sent a letter to the king of Israel requesting that he help Naaman. He does not mention Elisha in the letter. The Israel king thinks this is a trick to incite war when there was peace with Aram. Elisha hears about the letter and offers help. He reveals to Naaman the power of God and the land of Israel.

Despite being with Elisha, Gehazi did not learn proper behavior from him. His misbehavior shows what acceptable behavior is and that Naaman, an Aramean, is a better person than him.

We see the number seven emphasized again.

---

1. Midrash to Psalms 73:45; Flavius Josephus, *The Antiquities of the Jews,* volume 8, trans. William Whiston (Nashville, T.N.: Thomas Nelson, 2003). 15: 5

There are significant obscure items in the chapter. Did the king of Aram know of Elisha's abilities, which is why he sent his general to Israel? Is the story telling us that Israel's enemy Aram recognized Elisha's ability before the King of Israel did? Is this the first time that Elisha comes to the attention of Israel's king?

Secondly, are we being shown by how Elisha punishes Gehazi that Elisha is overzealous? Isn't the punishment of leprosy for the theft from Naaman overly harsh? Why are Gehazi's children punished?

Also, why doesn't Elisha deal with Naaman directly at first and not speak with him through his servant, Gehazi? Isn't this somewhat haughty? It did infuriate Naaman. It was only at the end that Elisha spoke directly to Naaman. Additionally, if he dealt with Naaman instead of having Gehazi do so, Gehazi would not have had an opportunity to steal from the Aramean general. Is the solution offered by many that Elisha was trying to show Naaman that he was not performing the cure, it was God, a good response?

Chapter 6

TWO PROPHECIES, TWO SEEMING MIRACLES, AND ONE TRICK

Chapter six has five of the twenty-nine Elisha activities. Elisha caused an axe-head to rise by penetrating it with a stick, prophesized an Aramean attack, prophesized the advance of their chariots, smote the Aramean army with blindness, and later restored their sight.

II KINGS CHAPTER 6

1. The budding prophets complained to Elisha, "The place where we used to live with you is too small for us.
2. Please, let's go to the Jordan. Every man should take a beam there, and let's build a place there to dwell." He answered, "Go."
3. One requested, "Could you please go with your servants." He replied, "I will go."
4. He went with them. When they came to the Jordan, they cut down wood.
5. But the axe-head dropped into the water as one cut a beam. He cried out, "Alas, my master! It was borrowed."
6. The man of God said, "Where did it fall?" He showed him the place. And he cut down a stick, threw it there, and made the iron swim.
7. Then he said, "Lift it." He stretched out his hand and took it.
8. Then, the king of Aram warred against Israel. He consulted with his servants and then instructed, "My camp will be in such and such a place."
9. The man of God sent to the king of Israel, saying, "Beware that you do not pass this place because the Arameans are coming there."
10. The king of Israel sent [someone] to the place the man of God told him and warned him of, and he guarded himself there, not once or twice.

11. The heart of the king of Aram was troubled over this thing. He called his servants and asked them, "Will you tell me which of us is for the king of Israel?"

12. One of his servants said, "None, my lord king. Elisha, the prophet in Israel, told the king of Israel the words you said in your bedroom."

13. He said, "Go and see where he is so I could send and take him." And he was told, "He is in Dothan."

14. Therefore, he sent horses, chariots, and a large army there. They came at night and surrounded the city.

15. When the servant of the man of God rose early and went out, [he saw] an army surrounded the city with horses and chariots. His servant said to him, "Alas, my master! What should we do?"

16. He replied, "Have no fear. For they that are with us are more than with them."

17. Elisha prayed, "Y-H-V-H, please, open his eyes, that he may see." And Y-H-V-H opened the eyes of the young man, and he saw the mountain was full of horses and chariots of fire round about Elisha.

18. When they came down to him, Elisha prayed to Y-H-V-H and said, "Please smite this people with blindness." And He smote them with blindness as Elisha requested.

19. Elisha said to them, "This is not the way nor the city. Follow me, and I will bring you to the man you seek. And he led them to Samaria.

20. When they came to Samaria, Elisha said, Y-H-V-H, open their eyes. And Y-H-V-H opened their eyes. They saw they were in Samaria.

21. The king of Israel asked Elisha when he saw them, "My father, should I smite them? Should I smite them?"

22. He answered, "Do not strike them. Would you smite those whom you took captive with your sword and bow? Place bread and water before them. When they finish eating and drinking, send them away so that they can return to their master."

23. He prepared abundant provisions for them. When they had eaten and drunk, he sent them away, and they went to their master. So, the bands of Aram stopped returning to the land of Israel.

24. But it came to pass after this that Ben-hadad, king of Aram, gathered his entire army and went and besieged Samaria.

25. And there was a great famine in Samaria. They besieged it until an ass's head was sold for eighty pieces of silver and the fourth part of a kab of dove's dung for five pieces of silver.

26. As the king of Israel was passing the wall, a woman cried to him, "Help, my lord the king."

27. He replied, "If Y-H-V-H doesn't help you, how can I help you? Out of the threshing floor or out of the winepress?"

28. And the king asked her, "What's bothering you?" She answered, "A woman said to me, 'Give me your son, that we can eat him today, and we will eat my son tomorrow.'

29. So we boiled my son and ate him. And I said to her the next day, 'Give me your son so we could eat him.' But she hid her son."

30. When the king heard the woman's words, he tore his clothes. He was passing the wall. People looked, and [saw] he wore sackcloth.

31. He said, "God do so and even more if the head of Elisha the son of Shaphat will remain on him today."

32. Meanwhile, Elisha sat in his house, and the elders sat with him. The king sent a man to him. But before the messenger came to him, he asked the elders, "Do you see how this son of a murderer sent to behead me? Look, when the messenger comes, shut the door and keep him at the door. Isn't the sound of his master's feet behind him?"

33. And while talking with them, the messenger arrived, and [the king] said to him, "This evil is from Y-H-V-H. Why should I wait for Y-H-V-H longer?"

COMMENTS ON THE CHAPTER

Slotki mentions the rational commentator Radak who explains that the stick had been previously cut and shaped to fit into the axe. This was no miracle. It is an example of Elisha's intelligence. He acted practically. He tossed the stick into the axe hole. This caused the axe to float.

Elisha then advised the king how he understood the Arameans would attack Israel. In verses 20 to 23, he shows consideration to the enemy soldiers.

In 24 to 31, we read about the horrors of King Ben-hadad's siege of Israel, behavior contrary to that of Elisha. The king of Israel frustratingly blames Elisha for the troubles. We do not know why. He seems to be overly cautious. He may have thought that Elisha's advice on how to react to Ben-hadad was foolish because it provoked the Arameans to take savage revenge. Alternatively, he might have thought Elisha did not do enough to ease the horrors, such as interceding with God.

Chapter 7

Chapter 7

ELISHA CONTINUES TO ADVISE ISRAEL'S KING

The chapter has three of the twenty-nine Elisha activities. He resolves the horrors performed by the Aramean army by prophesizing the end of the famine followed by an abundance of grain, and prophesizes that a military officer who mocked his prior prophecy would see how wrong he was.

II KINGS CHAPTER SEVEN

1. Elisha replied, "Hear what *Y-H-V-H* has to say. This is what *Y-H-V-H* said, 'Tomorrow, about this time, a measure of fine flour will be sold for a shekel, and two measures of barley for a shekel in Samaria's gate.'"

2. The captain on whose hand the king leaned answered the man of God, "[Even] if *Y-H-V-H* would make windows in heaven, could this happen?" He replied, "You will see it with your eyes but not eat it."

3. There were four leprous men at the entrance of the gate. They said to one another, "Why sit here until we die?

4. If we say we will enter the city, famine is in the city, and we will die there. If we sit here, we die also. So, come, let's go to the Aramean camp. If they save us, we will live. If they kill us, we will [simply] die."

5. So they rose at twilight and went to the Aramean camp. When they arrived at the edge of the Aramean base, [they saw] no one there.

6. For the Lord had made the Aramean army hear a noise of chariots and a noise of horses, a noise of a great host. They said one to another, "The king of Israel hired the king of the Hittites and the king of the Egyptians to come against us."

7. That's why they rose and fled at twilight, left their tents, horses, and asses, the camp as it was, and ran for their life.

8. When the lepers came to the camp's edge, they entered one tent, ate and drank, carried out silver, gold, and clothing, and left and hid it. Then they returned, entered another tent, took it from there, and went and hid it.

9. Then they said one to another, "We do not do enough today. It is a day with good results, yet we are silent. If we wait until morning, we will be punished. Therefore, let's go and tell the king's household."

10. So they came and called to the porters of the city. They told them, "We went to the Aramean camp and found no one there, no human sound, only horses tied, asses tied, and the tents as they were."

11. The porters called and told it inside the king's house.

12. The king rose that night and said to his servants, "I will now tell you what the Arameans did to us. They know we are hungry. So, they left the camp and hid in the field, planning, "When they leave the city, we will capture them alive and get into the city."

13. One of his servants answered, "Please let someone take five of the remaining horses, those left in the city. They are all that is left of the many that Israel had. They are just like the remnants of the Israelites that were consumed. And let us send [them out] and see."

14. So they took two chariots with horses, and the king sent [them] after the Aramean army, saying, "Go and see."

15. They went after them to the Jordan and [saw] that the entire way was full of garments and vessels that the Arameans tossed away in their haste. And the messengers returned and told the king.

16. So the people went and spoiled the Aramean tents. A measure of fine flour was sold for a shekel and two measures of barley for a shekel, as Y-H-V-H said.

17. The king appointed the captain on whose hand he leaned to oversee the gate. The people trampled him at the gate, and he died, as the man of God had said, who spoke when the king came down to him.

18. It happened just as the man of God told the king, "Two measures of barley for a shekel, and a measure of fine flour for a shekel, will be [the price] about this time tomorrow in Samaria's gate,"

19. and when the captain answered the man of God, "[Even] if *Y-H-V-H* would make windows in heaven, could this happen?" He replied, "You will see it with your eyes but not eat it."

20. This happened to him: people trampled him in the gate, and he died.

COMMENTS ON THE CHAPTER

The Babylonian Talmud *Sotah* 47a reports a rabbi's opinion that one of the four lepers in this chapter was Elisha's villainous former servant Gehazi whom Elisha cursed with leprosy. This is an interesting sermonic notion, but it is not hinted at in the text. Lepers were excluded from the community to avoid contamination, as mentioned in Leviticus 13:46.

The lepers reported their findings to the king of Israel who doubted their report. He feared that what the lepers saw was an Aramean trick to get the Israel force out of their safe area to where they could slaughter them.

Chapter 8

Chapter eight has three of the twenty-nine Elisha activities. Each is a prophecy. He prophesized a seven-year famine, King Ben-hadad's death, and that his successor Hazael would commit cruel acts against Israel.

II KINGS CHAPTER EIGHT

1. Then Elisha spoke to the woman whose son he had restored to life. He said, "Get up and go with your household and live where you want to live because *Y-H-V-H* called for a famine. It will last on the land for seven years."
2. The woman rose and did what the man of God said. She went with her household and dwelt in the land of the Philistines for seven years.
3. At the end of the seven years, the woman left the land of the Philistines and went to complain to the king concerning her house and land.
4. The king was talking with Gehazi, the servant of the man of God. He said, "Please tell me all the great things that Elisha did."
5. While he told the king how he had restored a dead body to life, the woman whose son he had restored to life cried to the king for her house and land. Gehazi said, "My lord king, this is the woman, and this is her son, whom Elisha restored to life."
6. When the king asked the woman, she told him. So, the king appointed a particular officer for her and said, "Restore all that was hers and all the fruits of the field since the day that she left the land until now."
7. When Elisha came to Damascus. Ben-hadad, the king of Aram, was sick. He was told that the man of God came.
8. The king said to Hazael, "Take a present in your hand, and go, meet the man of God, and ask him concerning *Y-H-V-H*, will I recover from this disease?"

9.   Hazael went to meet him. He took a present with him and every good thing of Damascus, forty camels' burden. He arrived, stood before him, and said, "Your son Ben-hadad, king of Aram, sent me to you to enquire, will I recover from this disease?"

10.   Elisha told him, "Go and tell him you will certainly recover. However, Y-H-V-H showed me that he would die."

11.   He glanced at him until *bosh* (a Hebrew word meaning ashamed, embarrassed, and a long while). And the man of God wept.

12.   Hazael asked, "Why are you crying, my lord?" He answered, "Because I know the evil you will do to the Israelites. You will set their strongholds on fire, slay their young men with swords, dash their children in pieces, and rip their pregnant women."

13.   Hazael responded, "Is your servant a dog who would do this terrible thing?" Elisha replied, "Y-H-V-H showed me you will be king of Aram."

14.   So he left Elisha. He came to his master, who asked him, "What did Elisha tell you?" He answered, "He told me that you would surely recover."

15.   He took a cloth the following day, dipped it in water, spread it over his face, and he died. And Hazael reigned in his stead.

COMMENTS ON CHAPTER EIGHT

Most of this chapter is obscure. We do not know why Elisha traveled to Damascus. It may be because he heard from God about Hazael and the need to act on this information, or he realized it intelligently. Verse 11 is unclear. Commentators disagree as to whom the first word "He" refers. It may be the future king Hazael who became "ashamed" when he realized that Elisha understood he would harm Israel when he assumed the throne. Alternatively, "He" is Elisha, who stared at Hazael with hatred and wept because he foresaw what Hazael would do, and Hazael became "embarrassed" by the steadfast stare. But the Hebrew *bosh* also means "a long while." Thus, verse 11 can be translated as, "*He* [Elisha] *glanced at him a long while, and the man of God wept.*" I prefer the third.

The Aramean King Ben-hadad requested Hazael to ask Elisha if he would recover from his illness. Elisha instructs Hazael to tell his king that Elisha predicted he would recover even though Elisha informs Hazael that Ben-hadad will die. Hazael reports to Ben-hadad that he will recover and does not reveal that

Elisha said he would die. Then Hazael placed a wet cloth over the king's face, and the king died.

Did Elisha tell Hazael to lie to his king? And if so, why? Did Hazael murder Ben-hadad by suffocating him? Did he seize the opportunity of Ben-hadad's illness to fool the Arameans into believing the king died of his illness?

Each episode is obscure. Readers must use their imagination to decipher the text and understand that what they think happened is only a guess.

I understand the following and admit I have no support for my view. I think Elisha told the truth. I see no basis for thinking he would lie. He told Hazael that Ben-hadad's illness was not serious. He could recover from it. But he saw the vicious character of Hazael and realized that he would seize the opportunity and murder the king.

Chapter 9

THE DEATH OF KING AHAB'S FAMILY

This chapter has one of the twenty-nine Elisha narratives. He prophesies that Jehu will murder King Ahab's family. King Jehu reigned over Israel from about 841 to 816 BCE. I write "about" because the dating in scripture is usually controversial because of such things as assigning the partial year of the death of a king to both the dead and the new king or just to the dead king.

II KINGS CHAPTER NINE

1. Elisha the prophet called one of the budding prophets and told him, "Here, take this vial of oil in hand and go to Ramoth-gilead;
2. When you come there, look for Jehu, son of Jeho-saphat, son of Nimshi, to make him leave his comrades, and take him to an inner chamber.
3. Then take the vial of oil, pour it on his head, and say, 'Yah-V-H said, I anoint you king over Israel.' Then open the door and flee. Don't hesitate.
4. The young man, the young prophet, went to Ramoth-gilead.
5. When he came, the military officers were sitting. He said, "I have some thing for you, sir." Jehu asked, "For which of us?" He replied, "You, sir."
6. He rose, went into the house, poured the oil on his head, and said to him, "Y[?]-V-H the God of Israel said, "I anointed you king over the people of Y-H-V-H, over Israel.
7. You will smite the house of Ahab, your master, that I may avenge the blood of my servants, the prophets, and the blood of all the servants of Y-H-V-H, through the hand of Jezebel.
8. For the entire house of Ahab will perish. I will cut off from Ahab every male, those shut up and at large.

Chapter 9

THE DEATH OF KING AHAB'S FAMILY

This chapter has one of the twenty-nine Elisha activities. He prophesizes that Jehu will murder King Ahab's family. King Jehu reigned over Israel from about 843 to 816 BCE. I write "about" because the dating in scripture is usually controversial because of such things as assigning the partial year of the death of a king to both the dead and the new king or just to the dead king.

II KINGS CHAPTER NINE

1. Elisha the prophet called one of the budding prophets and told him, "Hurry, take this vial of oil in hand, and go to Ramoth-gilead:
2. When you come there, look for Jehu, son of Jehoshaphat, son of Nimshi, go in, make him leave his comrades, and take him to an inner chamber.
3. Then take the vial of oil, pour it on his head, and say, 'Y-H-V-H said, I anoint you king over Israel.' Then, open the door and flee. Don't hesitate."
4. The young man, the young prophet, went to Ramoth-gilead.
5. When he came, the military officers were sitting. He said, "I have something for you, sir." Jehu asked, "For which of us?" He replied, "You, sir."
6. He rose, went into the house, poured the oil on his head, and said to him, "Y-H-V-H the God of Israel said, "I anointed you king over the people of Y-H-V-H, over Israel.
7. You will smite the house of Ahab, your master, that I may avenge the blood of my servants, the prophets, and the blood of all the servants of Y-H-V-H, through the hand of Jezebel.
8. For the entire house of Ahab will perish. I will cut off from Ahab every male, those shut up and at large.

9. I will make the house of Ahab like the house of Jeroboam, the son of Nebat, and like the house of Baasa, son of Ahijah.
10. Dogs will eat Jezebel in the portion of Jezreel. There will remain nothing to bury." Then he opened the door and fled.

The remainder of chapters 9 through 12 deal with the kings until chapter 13, when we hear about Elisha again.

COMMENTS ON CHAPTER NINE

Midrash Seder Olam identifies the then budding prophet with no support from the text as the famous Jonah ben Amittai. Elisha tells the youth to carry out the task, presumably because Elisha is too old to do so himself. He advises him to flee as soon as he completes the task because Jehu would kill him otherwise to ensure that no one knows he was anointed by an emissary of Elisha and what he intends to do.

Ahab's family were likely killed because they followed the evil ways of their parents.

Elijah foretold Elisha's prediction that dogs would consume Queen Jezebel's body in I Kings 21:23.

Chapter 10

ELISHA DIES

> This final chapter contains two of Elisha's activities on his deathbed and one after his death. The first two are straightforward. In the first, he prophesies that Israel's King Joash will destroy some Arameans. The second is inexplicable.

II KINGS CHAPTER 13

14. Elisha fell sick of a sickness where he would die. Joash, king of Israel, came to him, wept before him, and said, "My father, my father, the chariot of Israel and its horsemen."

15. Elisha said to him, "Take a bow and arrows." He took a bow and arrows.

16. Then he said to the king of Israel, "Place your hand on the bow." He put his hand, and Elisha set his hands on the king's hands.

17. Then he said, "Open the window facing east." He opened it. Then Elisha said, "Shoot." He shot. And he said, "The arrow is the *Y-H-V-H's* arrow of victory, the arrow of victory against Aram. You will defeat the Arameans in Aphek until you consume them."

18. Then he said, "Take the arrows." He took them. And he said to the king of Israel, "Strike them on the ground." He smote them thrice and stopped.

19. Then, the man of God became angry with him and said, "You should have struck five or six times. Then you would have smitten Aram until you entirely destroy it. Now, you will smite Aram just three."

20. Elisha died, and they buried him. Then, bands of the Moabites invaded the land at the year's outset.

21. As they were burying a man, they suddenly saw a band of men. They cast the man into the tomb of Elisha. As soon as the man touched the bones of Elisha, he revived and stood up on his feet.

COMMENTARY

We have no idea why Elisha should have become angry. He did not even hint to the king that he should smite the arrows five or six times. By saying "five or six," he seemed not to know the precise number. Additionally, this was not a proper way to address a king. This appears to be another instance of his impatience and overzealousness.

It is also unclear whether the acts done with the bow and arrows caused the enemy's defeat or only symbolized it. Also, did Elisha cause the defeat, or did the results of using the weapons show both Elisha and the king what would occur, a fact which they did not know before the king shot and struck the arrows?

The third act is where Elisha, now dead, revives a second person who was presumed dead. What is the author or authors telling us? Should we credit dead Elisha with this act? Or is this event telling us that Elisha was so important that such an event could occur even by touching his body? Are we expected to take this seriously? Or is the event, which is unnatural, even incredible, telling us to be suspicious of all former narrated Elisha events?

Even more significant is that the writer or writers of the Elijah episodes ended the narrations by leading us to understand that God was displeased with the prophet. They implied that taking him to heaven in a chariot is a metaphor for killing him. Yet here, Elisha is shown to perform a miracle after he dies. Are we being told that God approved of Elisha and he was superior to Elijah?

Elisha appears near the end of the reign of Israel's King Ahab. He dies just before Hazael becomes king of Aram. Thus, commentators state he prophesied between about 50 and 65 years. Ehrlich opts for 65. Cogan and Tadmor prefer "nearly a half-century."

Afterword

The Book of II Kings describes twenty-nine Elisha activities:

1. He parted the Jordan River (2:14)
2. Healed water by casting salt in it (2:21)
3. Killed forty-two children with two she-bears (2:24)
4. Insults Israel's king and the king's parents (3:13
5. Prophesized that a valley would be filled with water (3:17)
6. This prophesized water appeared to Moabites as blood (3:22)
7. Caused vessels to be filled with oil (4:4)
8. Prophesized that a Shunammite woman would have a son (4:16)
9. Resurrected this son by using various acts (4:34)
10. Cured a pottage by inserting meal (4:41)
11. Caused scant bread to be able to feed a hundred men (4:43)
12. Cured Naaman by having him bathe in the Jordan (5:14)
13. Could detect his servant Gehazi's theft (5;26)
14. Cursed Gehazi with Naaman's leprosy (5:27)
15. Caused an axe-head to rise by penetrating it with a stick (6:6)
16. Prophesized an Aramean attack (6:9)
17. Prophesized the advance of Aramean chariots (6:17)
18. Smote the Arameans with blindness (6:18)
19. Restored sight to the Aramean soldiers (6:20)
20. Prophesized the end of a famine (7:1)
21. Prophesized that a scoffing military officer could see what he doubted (7:2)
22. Prophesized that the Arameans would be deceived (7:6)
23. Prophesized a seven-year famine (8:1)
24. Prophesized Ben-hadad's death (8:10)

25. Prophesized Hazael's cruel acts against Israel (8:12)
26. Prophesized Jehu would murder King Ahab's family (9:7)
27. Prophesized Joash would destroy some Arameans (13:17)
28. Becomes angry at King Joash and prophesizes he would be unable to kill all the Arameans (13:19)
29. His dead body resurrects a dead man (13:21)

THE TWENTY-NINE BEHAVIORS CAN BE DIVIDED INTO FIVE CATEGORIES

1. Fourteen prophecies can be understood as communications from God or as Elisha using his human intellect without any aid from God to realize what will occur. The fourteen are 5, 6, 8, 16, 17, 20, 21, 22, 23, 24, 25, 26, 27, and 28.

2. Two instances where Elisha states something will happen if another thing is done. This is similar to magician stage tricks where the audience is prompted to look at the magician's left and, unnoticed, produces his result with his right. The two are 2 and 10.

3. Three clearly natural acts: 9 where he resurrects a child using artificial respiration, 13 where he can detect that his servant stole items, and 15 when he caught an axe-head by inserting a stick into it.

4. One instance, 29, where the Bible states his dead body revived a soldier's dead body when the latter touched his corpse.

5. There are eight seemingly unnatural activities where it is difficult, but not impossible, to say they were not miracles. They are 1, 3, 7, 11, 12, 14, 18, and 19. Two are similar to what Elijah did. Both split the Jordan River and caused oil to increase.

6. Four of the twenty-nine are acts where Elisha shows what appears to be human frailties, 3, 4, 14, and 28.

Elisha's lists of twenty-nine activities and seemingly unnatural ones exceed those of Elijah: twenty-nine acts for Elisha against twenty for Elijah, Eight seemingly unnatural ones for Elisha, and five for Elijah.

Why does Jewish tradition extol Elijah over Elisha? The Bible seems to be the opposite of tradition. It praises Elisha, not Elijah. The Bible implies that God was displeased with Elijah and took him to heaven, a symbolic way of saying He killed him. In contrast, it praises Elisha so much that his corpse resurrected a person after his death. So why does the prophet Malachi say that Elijah will announce the coming of the Messiah? Why is there a need for the Messiah to be announced? Didn't Maimonides say that the messianic age will be a natural period and the Messiah a natural human who will live and die as other people, and the only difference is that it will be a time of peace?" He said that prophecies such as a lion sleeping with sheep should be understood metaphorically as a time when people can coexist peacefully.

There are at least two possibilities.

(1) The idea that God was displeased with Elijah is wrong. God liked the zeal of Elijah who loved Him and felt Elijah was His faithful messenger. I do not think this is correct. I am convinced that the author or authors of the biblical book Kings preferred Elisha over Elijah. This is why Elisha is given more activities and more that are seemingly unnatural.

The second-century Hellenistic Jewish sage Ben Sira extols Elisha over Elijah because Elisha performed twice as many helpful activities.[1]

Similarly, centuries later, the Babylonian Talmud *Sanhedrin* 47a states that Kings 13:21 was written to praise Elisha. Babylonian Talmud *Chullin* 7b and Rashi on the Talmud text repeat what is in *Sanhedrin*. In *Sanhedrin*, Rabbi Papa says Elisha's miracle of resurrecting a dead man shows that while Elijah only revived one person, Elisha did two.[2] Rabbi Yochanan agrees that Elisha did more than Elijah but suggests he did so during his lifetime because a leper is considered a dead man, and Elisha cured him. In his commentary to *Chullin* 7b, Rashi praises Elisha by saying Elijah had to lie on the deceased child and do other things to the child, while just touching Elisha's corpse, resulted in the resurrection.

Y. Kiel agrees. He writes that II Kings 13:14 relates Elisha died from an illness to show that he was different than Elijah who was not sick. Although Kiel does not elaborate, he is likely hinting that God killed Elijah to remove him from his over-zealous treatment of the Israelites. Kiel praises Elisha by quoting Gersonides, who states, as Ehrlich did later, that Elisha was "The chariot of Israel and its horseman" because he battled for Israel by advising the king of Israel how to defeat Israel's enemy Moab, who used physical chariots and horsemen. Elisha

1.   R.W. Skehan and A. Di Lella, *The Wisdom of Ben Sira* (Doubleday, 1987), 529–530.
2.   The references are to I Kings 17:22 for Elijah and II Kings 2:9 for Elisha.

was equal to the Moabite military. Kiel also mentions that Gersonides suggests that the text should not be understood as a report of a resurrection. It could be interpreted as saying people removed the dead Aramean soldier's body from Elisha's tomb so that the dead enemy soldier's body would not desecrate it.

Ehrlich stresses that Malachi was the first person who praised Elijah. In his commentary to II Kings 2:11, he notes that no prophet mentions Elijah for centuries until the prophet Malachi does so. There is also no mention in the Hebrew Bible of anyone being taken to heaven because the Israelites did not think this was possible. Therefore, the words must be symbolic of death. We can add that even the budding prophets in II Kings 2 could not accept the notion that a chariot took Elijah to heaven. They went in search of his body.

What happened to his body? Ehrlich explains that the Torah generally refused to reveal the burial place of prophets lest superstitious people would visit their graves and petition the corpses to intercede with God to help them. This explains why Elisha refused to reveal Elijah's burial place to the young budding prophets. Unfortunately, despite the well-meaning precaution, many misguided Jews and non-Jews still today rush to graveyards of rabbis and saints and make petitions.

In short, multiple sources feel that Elisha, as Elijah prophesied, was twice as good as him.

(2) A second explanation as to why the book Malachi contends Elijah would announce the Messiah may be that Malachi or the author or authors of his book, who lived several centuries after Elijah and Elisha, invented the idea for personal reasons. We do not know Malachi's name or when he lived. He is called Malachi, which means "messenger of God." He identified himself with Elijah and saw him as a messenger of God with his mission to bring people to God and peace for the world. In his book 3:23–24 (4:5–6 in the Christian Bible), he states, "Behold, I will send you the prophet Eliyah before the great and terrible day of Y-H-V-H comes. He will turn the hearts of fathers to children and the hearts of children to fathers. Otherwise [if people continue to engage in strife], I will come and eradicate the land." In essence, he or the author or authors of his book gave Elijah the role of messenger that he saw in himself.

Why do I say that it could have been the author or authors of the book who originated the notion that Elijah, or more precisely Eliyah, would announce the coming of the Messiah? Robert C. Denton reveals the view of many scholars in *The Interpreter's Bible*[3] that the final two verses of Malachi were composed long after Malachi's death. The addition was "a late exegetical note intended to supplement the eschatology of 3:13–4:3 … where the coming of the Lord is preceded by the coming of his messenger, and also to identify the mysterious "messenger" with Elijah the prophet. The commentator who made the insertion presumably picked on Elijah because of the latter's ascension into heaven (II Kings 2:11), which would seem to make him available for this kind of mission. As a result of this bit of speculative exegesis, the figure of Elijah came to have a considerable role to play in later apocalyptic thought (cf. Ecclus. 48:10; Mark 6:15: 9:4, 11) and in rabbinical literature (Mishnah, *Baba Metzia* 1:8; 2:8; 3:4–5; *Eduyoth* 8:7). The commentator has changed the messenger's task somewhat from that which Malachi assigned in 3:3. He is not to prepare the Temple for the Lord's coming but to restore peace and social well-being to the community so as to avert God's wrath in the day of judgment."[4]

---

3. Denton, R.C. with exposition by W.L. Sperry *The Interpreter's Bible,* volume 6, The Book of Malachi (Nashville: Arlington Press, 1956).

4. I think Denton is correct. It should surprise no one that items were added to original biblical writings. This happened often. For example, the rabbis required that the next to last verse in Malachi be repeated after the last verse when the book is read in the synagogue so that the final book of the Bible does not conclude with a threat. To cite another example, many scholars are convinced that the last part of Kohelet (Ecclesiastes), verses 9–14, are editorial additions by a scribe who wanted to defend Kohelet from people who considered the book heretical. See A. Cohen, ed. *The Five Megilloth,* Ecclesiastes, introduction and commentary by V.E. Reichert (London: The Soncino Press, 1952), 189. These maneuvers were not unique to Judaism. In her brilliant translation of *The Odyssey,* Homer (W.W. Norton & Company, Inc., 2018), 72, Emily Wilson reveals that two Homeric scholars in the third and second centuries BCE argued that all of the poem after 23:295 and the entire last chapter 24 are not original parts of the poem. The book, they said, and many later agreed, ended with the words, "Finally, at last with joy, the husband and wife arrived back in the rites of their marriage bed."

Sources

Abarbanel, Rabbi Don Isaac. *Nevi'im Rishonim*. New York: Seforim Torah Vada'at, 1955.

Babylonian Talmud tractates: *Chullin, Sanhedrin, Sotah*.

Cogan, Mordechai, and HayimTadmor. *II Kings*, Vol. 11. Anchor Bible, 1988.

Cohen, A. ed. *The Five Megilloth*, Ecclesiastes, Introduction and Commentary by Victor E. Reichert. London: The Soncino Press, 1952.

Denton, R.C. with exposition by W. L. Sperry, *The Interpreter's Bible*, volume 6, The Book of Malachi. Nashville, Arlington Press, 1956.

Ehrlich, Arnold Bogumil. *Mikra Ki-Pheshuto* (The Bible According to Its Literal Meaning). Edited by Harry M. Orlinsky. New York: Ktav, 1901, 1969.

Foakes-Jackson, F.J. *The Biblical History of the Hebrews*, Legare Street Press, 2023

Gersonides (Levi ben Gershon). *Perush Ralbag, Nevi'im Rishonim bet*, Mossad HaRav Kook, 2008.

Hertz, Dr. J.H. *The Pentateuch and Haftorahs*. Additional Notes. London: Soncino Press, 1972.

Josephus, Flavius. *The Antiquities of the Jews*. Trans. William Whiston. Nashville, TN: Thomas Nelson, 2003. First published in 1737.

Kiel, Yehuda. *Sefer Divrei Hayamim bet*, Mossad Harav Kook, 1986.

_____. *Sefer Melachim*, Books one and two, Mossad Harav Kook, 1989.

Maimonides, Moses (Rambam). *Guide for the Perplexed*. Hebrew translation by Michael Friedlander. New York: Dover edition, 1956.

_____, *Guide for the Perplexed*. Translation by Shlomi Pines. Chicago: University of Chicago Press, 1963, digitized in 2010.

Malbim (Wisser, Meir Leibush ben Yehiel Michel), *Otzar Haperushim al Nakh, Mefarshei Hatanakh, undated.*

Midrash Seder Olam.

Olam Hatanakh, Divrei Hayamim, Melachim Aleph and Bet, 1999 and 2002.

Robinson, Joseph. *The First Book of Kings,* The Cambridge Bible Commentary Series, Cambridge University Press, 1972.

_____. *The Second Book of Kings,* The Cambridge Bible Commentary Series, Cambridge University Press, 1976.

Scriptures, Megillot, and Apocrypha sources (Pentateuch/Prophets/Writings): Deuteronomy, Exodus, Genesis, Joshua, I/II Kings, Leviticus, Luke, Malachi, Mark, Numbers, I Samuel.

Skehan, R.W. and A. Di Lella. *The Wisdom of Ben Sira,* Doubleday, 1987.

Slotki, Israel Wolf, *Kings.* London: The Soncino Press, 1950.

Steinsaltz, Rabbi Adin. *HaTanakh HaMevoar: Hamesh Megillot,* Koren Press, Jerusalem, 2017.

Wilson, E., *The Odyssey, Homer,* W.W. Norton & Company, Inc, 2018.

Index

Brigadier General Israel Drazin

EDUCATION: Dr. Drazin, born in 1935, received three rabbinical degrees in 1957, a BA in Theology in 1957, an MEd in Psychology in 1966, a JD in Law in 1974, an MA in Hebrew Literature in 1978, and a PhD with honors in Aramaic Literature in 1981. After that, he completed two years of post-graduate study in Philosophy and Mysticism. He graduated from the US Army's Command and General Staff College and its War College for Generals in 1985.

MILITARY: Brigadier General Drazin entered Army Active Duty at age 21 as the youngest US Chaplain ever to serve on active duty. He served on active duty from 1957 to 1960 in Louisiana and Germany and then joined the active reserves and soldiered, in increasing grades, with half a dozen units. From 1978 until 1981, he lectured on legal subjects at the US Army Chaplains School. In March 1981, the Army requested that he take leave from civil service and return to active duty to handle special constitutional issues. He was responsible for preparing the defense in the trial challenging the constitutionality of the Army Chaplaincy. The military chaplaincies of all the uniformed services, active and reserve, and the Veteran's Administration were attacked utilizing a constitutional rationale and could have been disbanded. The Government won the action in 1984, and Drazin was awarded the prestigious Legion of Merit. Drazin returned to civilian life and the active reserves in 1984 as Assistant Chief of Chaplains, the highest reserve officer position available in the Army Chaplaincy with the rank of Brigadier General. He was the first Jewish person to serve in this capacity in the US Army. During his military career, he revolutionized the role of military chaplains, making them officers responsible for the free exercise of rights of all military personnel, requiring them to provide for the needs of people of all faiths and atheists. General Drazin completed this four-year tour of duty with honors in March 1988, culminating in thirty-one years of military service.

ATTORNEY: Israel Drazin graduated from law school in 1974 and immediately began a private practice. He handled all suits, including domestic, criminal, bankruptcy, accident, and contract cases. He joined with his son in 1993 and formed offices in Columbia and Dundalk, Maryland. Dr. Drazin stopped actively practicing law in 1997 after twenty-three years.

CIVIL SERVICE: Israel Drazin joined the U.S. Civil Service in 1962 after his active duty service and remained a civil service employee, with occasional leave for military duty until retirement in 1990. At retirement, he accumulated thirty-one years of creditable service. During his US Civil Service career, he held many positions, including being an Equal Opportunity Consultant in the 1960s (advising insurance company top executives regarding civil rights and equal employment) and the head of Medicare's Civil Litigation Staff (supervising a team of lawyers who handled suits filed by and against the government's Medicare program). He also served as the director for Maryland's Federal Agencies' relationships with the United Fund.

RABBI: Dr. Drazin was ordained as a rabbi in 1957 at Ner Israel Rabbinical College in Baltimore, Maryland, and subsequently received *semichot* from two other rabbis. He entered Army active duty in 1957. He left active duty in 1960 and officiated as a weekend rabbi at several synagogues, including being the first rabbi in Columbia, Maryland. He continued the uninterrupted weekend rabbinical practice until 1974 and then officiated as a rabbi intermittently until 1987. His rabbinical career totaled 30 years.

PHILANTHROPY: Dr. Drazin served as the Executive Director of the Jim Joseph Foundation, a charitable foundation that gives money to support Jewish education, for just over four years, from September 2000 to November 2004.

AUTHOR: Israel Drazin is the author of over fifty books, some in the process of being published, more than 500 popular and scholarly articles, and over 10,000 book, movie, and music reviews that appear on Amazon and other sites. He wrote a book about the case he handled for the US Army, edited two books on legends by his father, children's books with his daughter, and many scholarly books on the philosopher Maimonides and the Aramaic translation of the Bible. His website is www.booksnthoughts.com, which contains over one thousand of his essays. He publishes weekly articles on this site and Times of Israel, the San Diego Jewish World, Goodreads, and Midwest Book Review.

LECTURES: Dr. Drazin delivered lectures at Howard Community College, Lynn University, and the US Army Chaplains School and continues to give talks to military chaplains.

MEMBERSHIPS AND AWARDS: Brigadier General Drazin was chosen in 2019 for the prestigious Albert Nelson Marquis Lifetime Achievement Award. He is admitted to practice law in Maryland, the Federal Court, and before the U.S. Supreme Court. He is a member of several attorney Bar Associations and the Rabbinical Council of America. He was honored with many military awards, including the RCA 1985 Joseph Hoenig Memorial Award and the Jewish Welfare Board 1986 Distinguished Service Award. Mayor Kurt Schmoke of Baltimore, Maryland, named February 8, 1988, "Israel Drazin Day." A leading Baltimore Synagogue called him "Man of the Year" in 1990. He is included in the recent editions of *Who's Who in World Jewry, Who's Who in American Law, Who's Who in Biblical Studies and Archaeology, Marquis Who's Who* of 2019, and other *Who's Who* volumes.